T0049321

Lady Gaga

Born to Be a Star

By Nicole Horning

Portions of this book originally appeared in
Lady Gaga by Claire Kreger-Boaz.

LUCENT
P R E S S

Published in 2020 by
Lucent Press, an Imprint of Greenhaven Publishing, LLC
353 3rd Avenue
Suite 255
New York, NY 10010

Copyright © 2020 Greenhaven Press, a part of Gale, Cengage Learning
Gale and Greenhaven Press are registered trademarks used herein under
license.

All new materials copyright © 2020 Lucent Press, an Imprint of Greenhaven
Publishing, LLC.

All rights reserved. No part of this book may be reproduced in any form without
permission in writing from the publisher, except by a reviewer.

Designer: Deanna Paternostro
Editor: Nicole Horning

Library of Congress Cataloging-in-Publication Data

Names: Horning, Nicole, author.
Title: Lady Gaga : born to be a star / Nicole Horning.
Description: New York : Lucent Press, [2020] | Series: People in the news |
    Includes bibliographical references and index.
Identifiers: LCCN 2019016690 (print) | LCCN 2019017241 (ebook) | ISBN
    9781534568303 (eBook) | ISBN 9781534568297 (library bound book) | ISBN
    9781534568280 (pbk. book)
Subjects: LCSH: Lady Gaga—Juvenile literature. | Singers—United
    States—Biography—Juvenile literature.
Classification: LCC ML3930.L13 (ebook) | LCC ML3930.L13 H67 2020 (print) |
    DDC 782.42164092 [B]—dc23
LC record available at https://lccn.loc.gov/2019016690

Printed in China

Some of the images in this book illustrate individuals who are models. The
depictions do not imply actual situations or events.

CPSIA compliance information: Batch #BW20KL: For further information contact Greenhaven Publishing LLC, New York,
New York, at 1-844-317-7404.

Please visit our website, www.greenhavenpublishing.com. For a free color
catalog of all our high-quality books, call toll free 1-844-317-7404 or fax
1-844-317-7405.

Contents

Foreword

We live in a world where the latest news is always available and where it seems we have unlimited access to the lives of the people in the news. Entire television networks are devoted to news about politics, sports, and entertainment. Social media has allowed people to have an unprecedented level of interaction with celebrities. We have more information at our fingertips than ever before. However, how much do we really know about the people we see on television news programs, social media feeds, and magazine covers?

Despite the constant stream of news, the full stories behind the lives of some of the world's most newsworthy men and women are often unknown. Who was Lady Gaga before she became a star? What does LeBron James do when he is not playing basketball? What inspires Lin-Manuel Miranda?

This series aims to answer questions like these about some of the biggest names in pop culture, sports, politics, and technology. While the subjects of this series come from all walks of life and areas of expertise, they share a common magnetism that has made them all captivating figures in the public eye. They have shaped the world in some unique way, and—in many cases—they are poised to continue to shape the world for many years to come.

These biographies are not just a collection of basic facts. They tell compelling stories that show how each figure grew to become a powerful public personality. Each book aims to paint a complete, realistic picture of its subject—from the challenges they overcame to the controversies they caused. In doing so, each book reinforces the idea that even the most famous faces on the news are real people who are much more complex than we are often shown in brief video clips or sound bites. Readers are also reminded that there is even more to a person than what they present to the world through social media posts, press releases, and interviews. The whole story of a person's life can only be discovered by digging beneath the surface of their public persona, and that is what this series allows readers to do.

The books in this series are filled with enlightening quotes from speeches and interviews given by the subjects, as well as quotes and anecdotes from those who know their story best: family, friends, coaches, and colleagues. All quotes are noted to provide guidance for further research. Detailed lists of additional resources are also included, as are timelines, indexes, and unique photographs. These text features come together to enhance the reading experience and encourage readers to dive deeper into the stories of these influential men and women.

Fame can be fleeting, but the subjects featured in this series have real staying power. They have fundamentally impacted their respective fields and have achieved great success through hard work and true talent. They are men and women defined by their accomplishments, and they are often seen as role models for the next generation. They have left their mark on the world in a major way, and their stories are meant to inspire readers to leave their mark, too.

Introduction

Mother Monster

In the 2018 film *A Star Is Born,* the character Rez Gavron says, "The queen is here!"[1] when Ally—played by Lady Gaga—walks into a room in one scene. It is the same thing thought by many fans who are lucky enough to see Lady Gaga in concert or what many think when they see her arrive at an awards show. To so many fans, she is an icon. She is also an advocate for marginalized groups, such as the LGBT+ community, and has spoken out in support of Black Lives Matter. She has even spoken out about her own health issues, such as fibromyalgia and post-traumatic stress disorder (PTSD). While many celebrities keep things such as health issues or their points of view to themselves, Lady Gaga does the opposite—she uses her platform to try to fight for acceptance and equality. As such, many fans view her as a role model and symbol of hope. Many people may feel like there is not a powerful voice to be an advocate for them, but Lady Gaga is open about things and communities of people she cares about. Additionally, the things that she cares deeply about also appear in her music. She does not shy away from speaking out about deep topics in her music, such as the song "Angel Down" from her album *Joanne*. The song is about the murder of Trayvon Martin, an unarmed black American teen who died when he was shot by George Zimmerman. In addition to being a powerful advocate who many fans look up to, she is an incredibly talented

Lady Gaga has staged public demonstrations to voice her social and political views, such as this protest in 2016.

singer, songwriter, and actress who commands the attention of her fans, also known as her Little Monsters, when she walks into a room.

Before the Fame

Lady Gaga was born Stefani Joanne Angelina Germanotta in 1986, and she was bullied from a young age—something that contributes to her being an icon and symbol of hope for others who have previously been bullied or are currently being bullied. Lady Gaga is proof that one can overcome terrible things that happen to them, such as being bullied for how one looks. When she started school at a private Catholic school in New York City, she was bullied constantly for how she styled her eyebrows and hair and for other aspects of her appearance. There were times that she did not want to even go to school because of how other people made her feel. These were hard times for her, and she credits them with giving her a drive to overcome obstacles. She said in an interview with Marissa Mayer of Yahoo, "Bullying really stays with you your whole life ... And it really, really never goes away. And I know you're using words like 'superstar' and 'most-Googled' and 'billions of YouTube [views].' But I was never the winner. I was always the loser. And that still stays with me."[2]

At age 11, she started taking vocal lessons from Don Lawrence, who was also pop singer Christina Aguilera's vocal coach. Additionally, she also took piano lessons and acting classes. These lessons prepared her for her later career as an actress, singer, and songwriter. After high school, she attended New York University's Tisch School of the Arts; however, she left the school in order to concentrate on performing. She had a large goal in mind and would not stop until it was achieved. In 2007, she was hired as a songwriter for pop stars such as Britney Spears and Fergie. She was composing hits for these stars and others when Akon—an R&B songwriter, singer, and record producer—heard her sing. He signed her to his label, and she finally got her break.

In 2008, her debut album *The Fame* was released, and she quickly became a household name with hit songs such as "Just Dance" and "Poker Face." Her next album, *The Fame Monster*, quickly followed in 2009. By this point, she had built a massive following, and with this massive following came two nicknames: fans call her "Mother Monster," and she calls them her "Little Monsters." These nicknames are part of the atmosphere that Lady Gaga creates in which her devoted fans feel like they are part of a diverse community and are welcomed no matter what. This was especially evident with the album *Born This Way*, which was released in 2011 and included empowering songs such as "Born This Way" and "Hair."

Lady Gaga is shown here at the Grammy Awards in 2010. She won awards for *The Fame* album and "Poker Face" and is wearing one of the over-the-top costumes she was known for in the early years of her career.

An Iconic Star

Lady Gaga's performances are exaggerated and theatrical. The sets are large, there are plenty of costume changes, and the atmosphere is one of fun and acceptance. Throughout her career, Lady Gaga has been known for her over-the-top performances and costumes, one of which was a dress made of meat that she wore to an awards show. An outsider may have thought that Lady Gaga's 15 minutes of fame were up around the time she released *ARTPOP* in 2013, which did not resonate with her fans as much as previous albums. However, her following grew as she took on additional roles and experimented with different sounds in her music.

Lady Gaga and Bradley Cooper are shown here performing the song "Shallow" from *A Star Is Born* at the Oscars in 2019. The song won an award at this ceremony for Best Original Song.

In 2014, she released an album called *Cheek to Cheek*, which included jazz duets with Tony Bennett. This was followed by roles on the television series *American Horror Story: Hotel* and *American Horror Story: Roanoke*. In 2016, her deeply personal album called *Joanne* was released and topped the charts. This album was named after her aunt, Joanne Germanotta, who passed away at a young age, and photos of her appear in the liner notes of the album. This same year, it was announced that a remake of the movie *A Star Is Born* was happening and that she was cast in it in the lead role of Ally. When the movie was released in 2018, it impressed audiences and critics, earning awards such as the Golden Globe and Oscar for the song "Shallow," which Lady Gaga sang with actor Bradley Cooper.

While costumes such as the meat dress have not been forgotten, Lady Gaga's fame reached a new level with this movie. She is not only a respected musician, she is also a respected actress and has proven over and over that she can take on different acting roles and music styles. She has proven that she is here to stay as an advocate, actress, singer, songwriter, and Mother Monster who her fans are devoted to.

Chapter One

The Star Is Born

Lady Gaga worked hard to be the award-winning singer, songwriter, and actress that she is today. Before becoming known to the world as Lady Gaga, she was born Stefani Joanne Angelina Germanotta on March 28, 1986, to parents Joe and Cynthia. On March 10,1992, Stefani's younger sister, Natali, was born. Joe and Cynthia fostered creativity in each of their children from an early age. In a 2018 interview with *InStyle*, Cynthia said they did this

> because we could see it. We could see the passion. We could see
> the joy that they gained from it, and we just made a decision to
> foster that. We were very [strict] with them about their school-
> work as well. I think it's really important to complete school and
> be well rounded in studies, so it was important for them to focus
> on that, but it was just very simple. There was such a passion
> and a joy for it and they were excelling at it so we fostered it.[3]

Convent of the Sacred Heart

Joe and Cynthia sent their daughters to a prestigious all-girl Catholic school, Convent of the Sacred Heart. Sacred Heart is located a couple of blocks from the Guggenheim Museum on

91st Street, on the Upper West Side of New York City. The exclusive private school demands of its students a rigorous academic schedule, but the administration also enforces a performing arts curriculum that begins in kindergarten and continues through high school. Sacred Heart requires each student to enroll in at least two music or drama classes and to perform in at least two school productions per academic year. Once in high school, girls are offered the chance to audition for two full-scale musical productions per year.

Stefani's passion for music was shown extremely early and in an unusual way when she learned how to play piano by ear. Her mother noticed this and asked if she wanted to take piano lessons. Cynthia said, "She was a little bit confused by that because she said that she heard the music in her head. She didn't understand why she had to take a lesson … that was a defining moment because I knew there was something different about her at that point. I didn't know what it would lead to, but I realized that there was something more there."[4]

Stefani's first piano recital occurred when she was just eight years old. She recalls the performance with affection and confidence: "I did a really good job. I was quite good."[5] In fact, Stefani was such a natural performer that her parents then enrolled her in daylong acting classes on Saturdays when she was 11 years old. Stefani immediately excelled in her drama classes. She vividly remembers her first acting lesson, in which she was asked to pretend to drink a cup of coffee. She attributes her dramatic ability both to these early classes and a heightened "sense memory" that allows her to intimately feel what she is trying to portray. As she has put it, "I can feel the rain [even] when it's not raining."[6]

Beginning in eighth grade, Stefani performed in several musical theater productions. She landed the lead in nearly every musical she auditioned for, including the lead role of Adelaide in *Guys and Dolls*. Fellow cast members recall that Stefani insisted that they call her by her character's name backstage and during rehearsals, which they found odd.

Lady Gaga has always had a close relationship with her family. She is shown here with her mother, Cynthia, and father, Joe, at an event with Tony Bennett (*far left*) for their duet album *Cheek to Cheek* in 2014.

Tragic Events

During her school years, Stefani was also bullied a lot. She was called names by her peers, and she was also thrown into a trash can by boys who lived down the block from her. She said in 2012, "I was called really horrible, profane names very loudly in front of huge crowds of people, and my schoolwork suffered at one point … I didn't want to go to class. And I was a straight-A student, so there was a certain point in my high school years where I just couldn't even focus on class because I was so embarrassed all the time. I was so ashamed of who I was."[7]

These feelings were made worse when she was 15 years old and two planes flew into the World Trade Center towers on September 11, 2001, killing nearly 3,000 people. She was shaken from this experience because of the tragedy of the event and fearing for her mother's safety. Her mother worked across the street from the towers, and Stefani did not know if she was okay after the attacks. Lady Gaga said in an interview many years later,

> I watched the towers fall from the roof of my school with my girlfriends. The whole city was covered in ashes. My dad picked me up and we couldn't reach my mom for ten hours. There was a television playing, we were all crying in the room. We went to the playground on the roof and the teachers were angry. We watched the towers fall from the roof because in New York, you could see them from any roof they were so big. I remember we were all crying. I remember leaving the school with my dad because we couldn't reach my mom. We saw all these guys from Wall Street covered in soot and all you could see was the water from their eyes from their tears.[8]

After these terrorist attacks against the United States, Stefani became extremely sad. One of the few places she felt comfortable was onstage, where she could express her creativity and lose herself in whichever character she played.

Born to Perform

Though she loved theater, music was Stefani's first love and the focus of her early arts education. She attributes her ability to write hit songs to the strict classical music training she received at Sacred Heart. "I was classically trained as a pianist and that innately teaches you how to write a pop song, because when you learn Bach inversions, it has the same sort of modulations between the chords," she said. "It's all about tension and release."[9]

Performing Arts Education

Being involved in performing arts stimulates creativity and also builds a sense of community among performing arts students. In addition to this, students learn the creative process, become more confident, learn how to collaborate with others, and build their focus in structured learning environments. Students with an interest in performing arts can take music lessons at school, and talented students with a deeper interest in music or acting can take additional classes after school or with a program in their area. For example, Lady Gaga took piano and acting classes when she was not at school.

Some performing arts centers have theater programs for high school students in which they can learn from professionals and get a head start in this area of study before going to college. Additionally, some performing arts centers may have summer camp sessions that help students develop their skills in ensemble performance. After high school, students can go to college for their area of interest to develop their skills. There are colleges that specialize specifically in performing arts such as music and theater, and there are also colleges with music programs.

Lady Gaga took music lessons outside of school and eventually went to college to study music, although she left in order to pursue a music career. Other famous people who have studied one of the areas of the performing arts include actor Chris Evans, who studied acting at the Lee Strasberg Theatre and Film Institute and went on to star as Captain America in the Marvel Cinematic Universe. Lin-Manuel Miranda took piano lessons and majored in theater studies at Wesleyan University. Miranda is the creator of the acclaimed musical *Hamilton*. Miranda also played the role of Alexander Hamilton from the show's debut in 2015 until 2016 and reprised his role in 2019 in Puerto Rico. In 2018, Miranda and Lady Gaga interviewed each other for *Variety* magazine.

Lin-Manuel Miranda (*right*) and Leslie Odom Jr. (*left*) are shown here performing in *Hamilton* in New York City's Richard Rodgers Theatre.

By the time she was 13 years old, Stefani had written her first piano ballad.

When she was 14 years old, Stefani regularly showed up at open mic nights to play her songs in front of audiences at nightclubs around New York City. She was almost always accompanied by her mother since she was too young to be admitted to the mostly 21-and-up venues. Cynthia wholeheartedly supported her daughter; in fact, she believed so deeply in Stefani's talent that she

Cynthia Germanotta (*left*) has fully supported her daughter's ambitions to work in the music industry and helped her develop her talents.

would promise club managers they would not be disappointed if they let her perform.

Stefani was instantly hooked on playing music before an audience. It was as though she was born to perform. However, the more she performed, the more she earned comparisons to other female singers and songwriters. Stefani did not care for these comparisons because she wanted to be known for her own talents and not as another version of someone else. She sought to distinguish herself by expanding her act to play with a full rock band. Therefore, at 16, Stefani formed a classic rock cover band that performed her favorite songs. Stefani's influences at the time included the Rolling Stones, Bruce Springsteen, Pink Floyd, Led Zeppelin, and the Beatles. In addition to performing with her cover band, Stefani also worked on writing original ballads, and in 2002, she recorded her first demo.

Tisch School of the Arts

All of Stefani's talent and hard work paid off in 2003 when, at 17 years old, she was one of 20 people in the world to receive early admission to the Tisch School of the Arts at New York University. Tisch is a highly competitive conservatory that specializes in the study of theater, dance, and film.

At Tisch, Stefani studied music and drama and wrote critical essays about art, religion, and social justice. She learned how to think critically about art and music, and she worked furiously to hone her songwriting skills. She also wrote a thesis on Spencer Tunick and Damien Hirst, two artists who deeply influenced her understanding of how to combine art with performance. Their graphic and shocking styles became ingrained in Stefani's consciousness and would later surface in her performance style.

After her second semester, she viewed studying performance as a waste of her talent and decided to quit Tisch to pursue a career in her true passion: music. Her parents were supportive of her decision. This time, however, there was a catch: If she did not succeed in music, she had to return to Tisch and finish her college degree, which she agreed to. During this time, she focused on what to do next and how to get to where she truly wanted to be.

Spencer Tunick and
Damien Hirst

Spencer Tunick is an American photographer who specializes in installations of large groups of people posed in urban spaces, in forests, and on beaches. Damien Hirst is a British artist whose art installations are often composed of dead animals preserved in formaldehyde and placed in large glass display cases. Both artists challenge viewers by bringing subjects such as death into public space. Their images are shocking and disturbing. Lady Gaga was heavily influenced by the artistic styles of these two men.

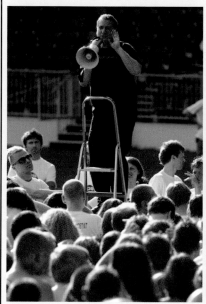 

Spencer Tunick (*left*) and Damien Hirst (*right*) are shown here with their art installations. Their unique art has heavily influenced Lady Gaga's music, fashion, and shows.

Booking Gigs

While being on her own and figuring out how to make a career out of her passion, Stefani worked as a waitress at the Cornelia Street Café. She also continued performing with her band, called the SGBand. The band performed in several clubs, including the Bitter End. While booking the band, she would pretend to be the band's publicist and pitch them to the booking agents at the club. Kenny Gorka, who was a booking agent for the Bitter End at that time, said, "She lied to me, talking about how great Stephani [sic] was in the third person … But it was enough to pique my interest, and I brought her in for an audition and booked her."[10] She was determined to get the band gigs and turn her passion into a career. With each performance, she was getting closer and closer to becoming Lady Gaga.

Chapter Two

The Fame Monster

The year after leaving Tisch was an uncertain one for Stefani Germanotta. She did not want to get forced back into going to Tisch, but getting her career in music to take off was difficult. However, it was during this time that she met important people who would become instrumental to both her transformation into Lady Gaga and to the success of her award-winning debut album, *The Fame* and its successor, *The Fame Monster*.

"It" Girl

Germanotta was able to focus on her music full-time once she did not have to attend classes or complete homework assignments. During the day, she worked at an internship for Famous Music Publishing, where she made copies of press releases and performed other administrative tasks. By night, she continued to perform in nightclubs with the SGBand. One evening in January 2006, her band was playing in the same club as singer and talent scout Wendy Starland. She and Starland had met once before, when Starland visited the Famous Music Publishing offices to speak with Germanotta's boss. Germanotta confessed to being a fan at their first meeting and told Starland she had been listening to one of her songs repeatedly. At the time, Germanotta did not

Rob Fusari was looking for a female vocalist and was introduced to Lady Gaga. He later credited himself with having the idea for the name "Lady Gaga."

leave a lasting impression on Starland. In fact, when Germanotta approached her the night they were to play in the same club, Starland had low expectations for her performance.

The night the SGBand shared a stage with Starland turned out to be a turning point in Germanotta's career. Starland remembers thinking that the SGBand was terrible, but once she heard Germanotta sing, she was floored by her raw talent. Germanotta did not know it, but Starland had been tasked by producer Rob Fusari with finding a strong female vocalist for an upcoming project. Germanotta's voice, energy, and piano skills had Starland on the phone to Fusari that very night. She called the producer to tell him she had found his next "it" girl.

A Mysterious Origin Story

When Fusari first met Germanotta, he doubted she would turn out to be the powerhouse rock vocalist he was searching for. However, Fusari immediately recognized that Germanotta was special when she played a song she wrote on the piano. "In

20 seconds," Fusari said, "I knew this girl would change my life."[11] They decided to work together and formed a close bond.

There are several stories about how Germanotta got the name Lady Gaga, and there has been a lawsuit over it. First, Germanotta credits Fusari with coming up with the "Gaga" portion of the name. It is reported that the "Lady" part was created by Germanotta because she had been using her real name for so long and wanted a change. Another version states that in one of Fusari's text messages to Germanotta in which he meant to reference the Queen song "Radio Ga Ga," his phone autocorrected the words to "Lady Gaga" and Germanotta loved it. In 2010, Fusari sued Germanotta for $30 million, claiming she had cut him out of a business deal and he was to be credited with the creation of her name. Yet another version of her name creation states that the name "Lady Gaga" was invented by recording business executives in a marketing meeting.

A Successful Meeting

The pieces were starting to come together, and Lady Gaga was more driven than ever to define her musical style and write a hit song. Most of the songs she and Fusari wrote were hard rock or grunge, which sounded all wrong to Fusari. Though he originally sought a female lead rock vocalist, the style did not adequately showcase Lady Gaga's talent. He proposed they switch gears and try to write pop songs with a dance beat. Lady Gaga agreed, and in one day, they wrote the song "Beautiful, Dirty, Rich," which was later included on her album *The Fame*.

Fusari knew they had a hit with "Beautiful, Dirty, Rich." He sent the recording to record executive Joshua Sarubin at Island Def Jam. Sarubin immediately set up a meeting between Lady Gaga, Fusari, and Def Jam chair Antonio "L.A." Reid. Lady Gaga nailed the audition, and Reid noted that she would likely transform pop music for women with her outlandish style and powerful vocals. However, for reasons unknown, the partnership between Lady Gaga and Def Jam lasted just three months before she was dropped from the label. She was devastated by the rejection and briefly considered giving up on becoming a star. Fusari

Once *The Fame* was released, Lady Gaga worked hard to promote the album. She is shown here performing in 2008.

encouraged her to take a short break and spend time with her family while he considered their next move.

Shortly after this, Fusari introduced Lady Gaga to producer RedOne, who would eventually cowrite her popular hits "Just Dance," "Boys Boys Boys," and "Poker Face." The successful meeting between Lady Gaga and RedOne energized Fusari to secure another recording contract. He contacted his friend Vincent Herbert from Streamline Records, a division of Interscope Records. Herbert recognized Lady Gaga's star power and signed the budding superstar to her second major record label—all by the time she was 19 years old.

Lady Gaga's Early Work

The Portal in the Park is a children's book by Cricket Casey published in 2006. The book contains a CD featuring Grandmaster Melle Mel rapping the book's narration, and a then-unknown Lady Gaga sings on two tracks: "World Family Tree" and "The Fountain of Truth." Casey asked her to participate in the project after seeing the pre-Gaga Germanotta perform at New York's Bitter End. The original printing of the book has only a minor mention of Lady Gaga, but subsequent printings feature her prominently.

Lollapalooza

Around this time, Lady Gaga met bar manager Luc Carl, and they soon began dating. Through him, she met Lady Starlight, a hard-rock disc jockey (DJ) at a bar Carl managed. The ladies made an immediate connection at Lady Gaga's 20th birthday party, where they decided to combine their shows into one act. They performed Lady Gaga's songs, with Lady Starlight as beat master and DJ.

Their tribute to 1970s-era variety acts gained popularity and eventually won them a spot at the Lollapalooza music festival in Grant Park in Chicago, Illinois, in 2007. Other acts at the festival that year included Pearl Jam, Modest Mouse, Amy Winehouse, and the Yeah Yeah Yeahs. The ladies recognized this as a great opportunity, and they jumped at the chance to perform for such a large audience.

Then unknown to the majority of the Lollapalooza audience, Lady Gaga made an impression with her already extravagant outfits as well as her talents. However, many people in the crowd confused the dark-haired Gaga with Amy Winehouse,

Lady Gaga is shown here performing at Lollapalooza in 2007. She was told after the performance to dye her hair blonde so she would not get confused with the singer Amy Winehouse, and she has mostly kept her hair blonde since then.

who was scheduled to perform the next night. Herbert, who had used his own money to send Gaga to Lollapalooza, was concerned that she would forever be confused with Winehouse if she did not immediately change her look. He told her to dye her dark hair blonde to save her career, which she did without question.

Expanding Her Reputation

After her well-received Lollapalooza performance, Lady Gaga learned that the record industry was a tight-knit community where everybody knew each other. This could either work for or against an artist, but in Lady Gaga's case, it was beneficial to her career. She was able to use her internship with Famous Music Publishing to get a job writing songs for established artists at Interscope. This was a key career move that expanded her reputation among record executives.

NKOTB

Lady Gaga was the opening act for New Kids on the Block (NKOTB) during their 2008 reunion tour. She had been signed to Interscope Records, and NKOTB were label mates. Gaga was commissioned to write material for their album *The Block*. She wrote and appeared as a featured guest on the track "Big Girl Now" and also toured with NKOTB from October to November 2008 to promote her first major release, *The Fame*.

In the spring of 2007, Sony/ATV Music Publishing signed a publishing deal with Lady Gaga. This contracted her to write songs for performers such as Britney Spears ("Quicksand"), New Kids on the Block ("Big Girl Now"), and more. Jody Gerson, who signed the publishing deal between Lady Gaga and Sony/ATV, immediately recognized Gaga's star power. She said of meeting her, "She blew me away from the moment I met her."[12] At last, Lady Gaga felt like industry insiders were beginning to notice her.

Lady Gaga Gets Discovered

Lady Gaga worked tirelessly to make the right connections. She continued to write songs for other artists, work on her own music, and collaborate with any artist she could. Once again, Lady Gaga's determination paid off when she caught the attention of R&B performer/producer Akon. Lady Gaga sang guide vocals for one of his songs (guide vocals, or reference vocals, act as a place holder for lyrics yet-to-be-recorded to show how the pitch and melody should sound), and Akon immediately appreciated Lady Gaga's powerful voice. His instincts told him that she was far too talented to remain a reference vocalist, and he wanted to help her become a star. He quickly obtained permission from Interscope chair Jimmy Iovine to sign Lady Gaga to his label, Kon Live Distribution. Akon was an early believer that she was destined to be a megastar, and he said of meeting her, "She was definitely a blessing. She came at the right moment. I'm glad I believed in her, boy."[13]

Once Gaga was under Akon's umbrella, she had access to all the people and recording equipment necessary to record her first album, *The Fame*. She reconnected with RedOne, and together with Rob Fusari, Akon, and producer Martin Kierszenbaum, they wrote nearly all the songs for the album in just one week. *The Fame* included a staggering number of soon-to-be smash hits, such as "Just Dance," "Poker Face," "Paparazzi," "Beautiful, Dirty, Rich," and "LoveGame." Gaga composed the songs on the piano first and then sang the vocals for all the tracks in one take. She then went back and spent just a few hours recording the harmonies for each song. Everyone who worked with her on the album was amazed by how effortlessly the music flowed from her.

Lady Gaga, however, was not surprised by the speed with which *The Fame* came together. After all, she had worked on early versions of many of the album's songs for years before they were recorded. She always knew she would write a hit record and has said of the experience, "A hit record writes itself. Once you tap into the soul, the song begins to write itself."[14]

"Just Dance"

Interscope released *The Fame* on August 19, 2008, to mostly critical acclaim. Dance music fans around the world devoured the first single, "Just Dance," which was released months before the full-length album. The song became a dance anthem in night-clubs around the globe, but especially in gay dance clubs.

Most of the album's initial success occurred abroad in the United Kingdom, Australia, Ireland, and Canada. It took longer for the record to catch on in the United States. American critics gave the album mixed reviews, but Gaga was undeterred. Instead, she launched an exhaustive campaign to promote the album. Gaga's promotional assault included television performances on *So You Think You Can Dance*, *Jimmy Kimmel Live!*, *The Tonight Show with Jay Leno*, *The Hills*, and the Miss Universe beauty pageant. She also performed as the opening act for New Kids on the Block during the North American leg of their Live! tour in the fall of 2008.

Lady Gaga was finally in a position to reveal her superstardom to the world. She was determined to top the charts worldwide and show her critics that she was no flash-in-the-pan pop star. The savvy entertainer knew she must not rest or become comfortable with her success. Rather, she used her early success as motivation to work harder to prove to the world that Lady Gaga was here to stay.

Lady Gaga relentlessly promoted *The Fame* throughout the fall of 2008 and into 2009, including touring with NKOTB. These decisions paid off in record sales, positive reviews, and an exponential increase in her fan base. With each live performance, Gaga's record sales increased, as did her critical acclaim.

In 2009, the overwhelmingly positive response from critics and fans to *The Fame* eventually catapulted Lady Gaga's music to the top of the charts in the United States. By the end of the year, she had five top-ten songs on *Billboard* magazine's Top 100 list.

Lady Gaga toured with New Kids on the Block in 2008. Even in these early performances, she was showcasing her extravagant style, which would end up becoming as well-known as her songs.

She did not stop there—she began her first solo world tour and released her second album while the first was still dominating the airwaves.

Lady Gaga's Solo Tours

On March 12, 2009, Lady Gaga kicked off her first solo world tour at the House of Blues in San Diego, California. In less than 30 days, she headlined more than 19 concerts. Each show sold out quickly, and in many cases, additional seats and shows had to be added to accommodate the fans who wanted to see Lady Gaga live. The Fame Ball tour lasted just six months, but

Lady Gaga performed more than 70 shows throughout North America, Asia, and Europe.

The tour received mostly positive reviews from critics, even from those who had previously doubted Gaga's pop music significance. Jill Menze of *Billboard* wrote, "Lady Gaga has proven herself to be an of-the-moment pop sensation. Dig deeper, and it's clear she's versatile and talented enough to have staying power."[15] Not all reviews were glowing, however. Whitney Pastorek of *Entertainment Weekly* criticized Lady Gaga, and especially criticized her interactions with the audience.

Negative reviews of her performances were rare, though. Lady Gaga's commitment to theatrics, her powerful vocals, her piano-playing skills, and her sheer creativity forced critics to admit that she was a tour de force. Lady Gaga, however, was less concerned with pleasing critics and more interested in cultivating a relationship with her fans.

Gagavision

In June 2008, months before her debut album was released, Lady Gaga began a weekly web series about her quest to become a cultural phenomenon. Called *Transmission Gagavision*, the series comprised 40 episodes and ran through March 2009. Each broadcast began with the tagline "Lady Gaga has been sent to Earth to infiltrate human culture one sequin at a time."[1] The episodes took the form of a behind-the-scenes look at the life of Lady Gaga and served as an invitation to fans to take part in her ascent to global stardom. *Transmission Gagavision* was briefly started up again in 2011 for five episodes but has not aired since then.

1. Lady Gaga, "Lady Gaga—Transmission Gagavision," YouTube video, 2:08, posted August 15, 2008. www.youtube.com/watch?v=5-cx55NpKu4.

To this end, Lady Gaga launched the Monster Ball tour, which kicked off on November 27, 2009, in Montreal, Canada. Every show immediately sold out. As with the Fame Ball tour, most cities added extra dates, booked larger venues, and added more seats to accommodate her expanding fan base. When Lady Gaga kicked off her first tour at the House of Blues in San Diego, she played for about 1,000 people. When she went back to play the San Diego Sports Arena just nine months later, the seating

Lady Gaga did not sit and enjoy her initial success. She immediately went on two solo tours and started work on her second album. She is shown here on the Monster Ball tour.

capacity had to be increased from 6,000 to 10,800 seats. Later shows in larger venues that held more than 35,000 people sold out almost immediately after tickets went on sale.

Elaborate Performances

Lady Gaga quickly became known as an elaborate and outlandish performer who pushed the envelope of modern musical entertainment. She earned this reputation in 2009 with a succession of increasingly outrageous performances.

She first sent shock waves through the American entertainment industry when she appeared in an elimination episode of *American Idol* in April 2009. The eccentric singer performed her hit single "Poker Face" beneath pink stage lights and played a clear piano filled with bubbles. Once the song hit its groove, she danced her routine while wearing a space-age outfit complete with a zipper eye patch.

Gaga's appearance on *American Idol* made her one of the most sought-after guest entertainers on hit television shows throughout 2009. With each appearance, her performances became more theatrical, her costumes more outrageous, and her sets more elaborate.

Her trademark theatrics were also on full display at the 2009 MTV Video Music Awards (VMAs), where Lady Gaga was nominated for several awards—called Moonmen after their design—and also performed "Paparazzi" during the show. The millions of viewers who tuned in to the VMAs were treated to one of Gaga's most talked-about performances. Her stage was framed by an elaborate Gothic background with an ornately decorated giant staircase. Her set opened with the crashing sound of an enormous, fallen crystal chandelier, with Lady Gaga lying in its wreckage. Backup dancers dressed in white twirled around her and raised her up as she sang.

She wowed the star-studded audience when she banged furiously on her white piano, with one leg propped up on the keys. The truly shocking moment came, however, toward the end of the song when fake blood suddenly poured down Lady Gaga's body and she was suspended in the air by her arm above the

Lady Gaga's first VMAs performance was successful and cemented her as a star in the music industry. Her performance was widely talked about, and she ended the night walking away with three awards.

stage. A triumphant Lady Gaga went on to win three VMAs: Best Art Direction and Best Special Effects for her "Paparazzi" video, and Best New Artist.

Leaving Fans Speechless

Just over a year after her debut album was released, *The Fame Monster* was released in November 2009. The album was a reissue of the first and also included additional songs. These additional songs would later be released as a standalone EP. Lady Gaga aggressively promoted *The Fame Monster* even before its release. In the weeks leading up to the album's official release, the first single from the album, "Bad Romance," had fans and critics buzzing about what the rest of the album might sound like.

The album was well received, and the music review website Pitchfork ranked "Bad Romance" at number 39 in their top 100 singles from 2009. Reviewer David Drake lauded Lady Gaga in his review when he said, "'Bad Romance' was the moment where the music didn't just live up to the (self-inflated) hype, but surpassed it. The track is epic in construction."[16] Lady Gaga's appeal was catching on as fans and critics alike realized that she was an indomitable performer who had no intention of slowing down.

In November 2009, Lady Gaga performed at the American Music Awards in Los Angeles, California. Though she was nominated for several awards, she did not win in any category, which surprised critics and disappointed fans. However, Lady Gaga stole the night with her stunning performance of "Bad Romance" and "Speechless."

Lady Gaga wore a flesh-colored bodysuit with white, glowing ribs as she dominated the ultramodern set with her dance routine. When she transitioned from "Bad Romance" to "Speechless," she used her microphone stand to smash a large glass box that encased her piano. She crawled into the box and started playing "Speechless" while the piano was on fire. Violinists who accompanied Lady Gaga wore gas masks and stood in other glass enclosures. Gaga took her exhibition even further when she smashed one glass bottle after another against her piano to accentuate the drama of her performance. The performance cemented Gaga's place as one of the most groundbreaking entertainers of her time.

Lady Gaga's popularity went viral once radio stations, dance clubs, and popular television shows began to play her music regularly. Her first single, "Just Dance," went four times platinum in December 2009 after it sold more than 4 million copies. The dance anthem spent five months on *Billboard* magazine's Hot 100 list, during which time her second single, "Poker Face," also made the hit list. Lady Gaga became the first artist in more than a decade to have two consecutive singles on the Hot 100. "LoveGame" and "Paparazzi" also made the list while the other songs were still on it, making her the unofficial queen of *Billboard* magazine's Hot 100. In fact, as of 2019, *The Fame* has the distinction of remaining in the number one slot on the Billboard Dance/Electronica Albums chart longer than any other album in history, a position which it held for 106 weeks.

Lady Gaga put on a memorable performance of "Bad Romance" and "Speechless" at the American Music Awards. During her performance of "Speechless," her piano started on fire while she continued to play.

Lady Gaga broke more records at the 2010 MTV Video Music Awards, where she set the record for the most nominations in the history of the VMAs, with 13 nominations. She accepted the award for the show's top honor, Video of the Year, for her "Bad Romance" video. Lady Gaga not only took the biggest award of the night, but also left with seven others.

The Bond with Her Little Monsters

With the awards and how often her songs were played on the radio, Lady Gaga's fan base exponentially grew. Fans were drawn to how different she was—she was not like other musicians in the industry. Her clothes were out of the ordinary, she put on thrilling performances, she was incredibly creative and talented, and her music was catchy. While touring in 2009, Lady Gaga starting calling fans "Little Monsters" because of how they would dance and scream in the stadiums. This created a special relationship between the singer and her fans, as well as among the fans themselves.

While giving fans a collective nickname was largely done in K-pop (a genre of pop music that originated in South Korea), it was not common in American music before Lady Gaga. This created a fandom, which is a subculture made up of fans of one particular thing, such as Marvel, *Star Wars*, *Harry Potter*, or *Doctor Who*. For example, fans of *Doctor Who* are called Whovians. While fans of movie or book series were commonplace, a nickname for such a large group of fans of a musician was completely new at that time. It created a special bond between Lady Gaga and her fans, and the fans felt like they had a bond between themselves, almost like an extended family. While outsiders might have viewed the bond and the singer as passing fads that would fizzle out at some point, they did the exact opposite. As Lady Gaga's popularity grew, the bond grew tighter and more personal. Lady Gaga would frequently post personal things such as photos on Twitter while other performers were only doing promotional posts at that time. Additionally, Lady Gaga started using a "monster claw" hand gesture that involved curled fingers and looked like a paw. With this, the phrase "paws up"

Lady Gaga is shown here using the monster claw hand gesture. Her "Little Monsters" tattoo dedicated to her fans is shown in the inset.

became popular at concerts between fans and Lady Gaga herself. She had created a community that was bonded by their love for their favorite performer. Additionally, this community could relate to the feelings of being an outsider that Lady Gaga often spoke about. The bond between the singer and her fans was solidified even more by Lady Gaga getting "Little Monsters" tattooed on the arm she uses to hold the microphone. She dedicated the tattoo to her fans on Twitter soon after she had it done. Her Twitter post included a link to a picture of the tattoo with the tweet, "look what i did last night. little monsters forever, on the arm that holds my mic. xx"[17]

Lady Gaga was selling out her tours, had released two albums, and gained a following of fans who followed her every move and looked to her style for inspiration. Both the music industry and fans anxiously waited for what Lady Gaga would do next, whether it was music or fashion choices.

Chapter Three

A Charitable and Fashionable Star

Lady Gaga's first album was released in 2008, and a reissue with additional material followed in 2009. While the reissue album followed quickly, it would be a while before her next album would be released. *Born This Way* would be released in 2011, and during this time between albums, Lady Gaga continued to build her fan base by touring, attending awards shows with her customary unique fashion, supporting charitable organizations, and standing up for people's rights.

Fashion!

Lady Gaga is widely recognized for her unique wardrobe. Some of her outfits have included tall, heel-less hoof boots. She often wears wigs and a variety of hats and has even arrived to an awards show on a large fake horse. Her costumes often feature bizarre, even unnerving, fabrics or items. For example, she raised eyebrows when she accepted the 2009 Best New Artist MTV Video Music Award dressed in a red lace ensemble that completely covered her face. She also created one of the most photographed meetings ever for the paparazzi when she greeted Queen Elizabeth wearing a red latex dress and sparkling red see-through eye patches. Though many people consider Lady Gaga's fashion sense to be over the top, even ridiculous, some clothing designers are inspired to create unusual outfits for her. Indeed, her style, celebrity, and willingness to take fashion risks make Lady Gaga fun to dress.

Designers who have created outfits for Lady Gaga include Alexander McQueen, Chanel, Viktor & Rolf, Jean Charles de Castelbajac, and Giorgio Armani. Lady Gaga most often dons Armani's creations at big, high-profile events, such as at the Grammy Awards, at the Metropolitan Museum of Art's Costume Institute Gala (also known as the Met Gala), onstage during the Monster Ball tour, and on *American Idol* in May 2010.

Armani particularly enjoys outfitting Gaga because of her free spirit and ability to wear just about anything. For example, one of the costumes Armani designed for Lady Gaga's 2010 Grammy Awards appearance was a stunning lavender hoop dress. The outfit included glittery stockings and arm coverings and was topped off by glittery high-heeled shoes. The shoes featured a barely-there heel that was sculpted in toward the front platform of the shoe, which was also a very tall platform. Their shared vision for fantasy couture has allowed Lady Gaga and Giorgio Armani to create unforgettable fashion statements.

An Inspiration for McQueen

It was Lady Gaga's relationship with designer Alexander McQueen, however, that most often caught the media's attention. McQueen's controversial designs naturally made him gravitate toward the eccentric Lady Gaga. The unconventional designer, who also worked with David Bowie, Rihanna, and Björk, created dark, even grotesque couture. Lady Gaga was attracted to—and influenced by—McQueen's gothic designs, which often included corsets made from animal bones and skins, feathers, lace, and extremely high-heeled shoes and boots. One of his most famous creations donned by Lady Gaga was the see-through red lace ensemble that she wore at the 2009 MTV Video Music Awards.

Lady Gaga has been photographed hundreds of times in McQueen originals, and all the outfits incorporated some or all of his signature materials. For a while, it seemed as if she wore

Lady Gaga is shown here on the Grammy Awards red carpet in 2010. Her hoop outfit was designed by Armani, and the heels of her shoes were sculpted in closely to the front platforms, showcasing the gravity-defying shoe style that Lady Gaga is well-known for wearing.

Lady Gaga is shown here wearing an outfit designed by McQueen at the MTV VMAs in 2010. He had died just a few months earlier.

only McQueen.

The trendy pair seemed to affirm this observation when they teamed up for Lady Gaga's "Bad Romance" video. In it, she sported McQueen's bejeweled lobster-claw shoes—10-inch (25.4 cm) stiletto heels with the foot rounded downward—for the first time. The shoes sent a ripple through the fashion industry when several models refused to wear them on the runway. The extremely uncomfortable, remarkably high heels caused the models to fear they would fall on the catwalk. Lady Gaga, however, was undeterred. In fact, all the outrageous outfits and footwear Lady Gaga wears in the "Bad Romance" video were created by McQueen. Their connection was so strong that the designer's publicist referred to Gaga as McQueen's "unofficial Muse."[18] Thus, Gaga was among those most devastated when the 40-year-old designer died by suicide in February 2010.

Lady Gaga's Style Squad

Though Lady Gaga is a magnet for high-profile fashion designers to test daring new clothing lines, the majority of her costumes are designed in-house. In yet another expression of her desire to be unique, Lady Gaga has assembled a creative team to help her remain on the cutting edge of the entertainment industry. This group of designers, artists, inventors, and tech personnel are collectively known as the Haus of Gaga.

The Haus of Gaga is responsible for all things Lady Gaga. The collective is divided into creative teams that each work to enhance, support, and reinvent her image, style, and live performances. Lady Gaga's goal in assembling the team was to combine all aspects of art, music, and performance to form a complete entertainment package. The sole purpose of the Haus is to realize Lady Gaga's wildest fantasies through couture, props, short films, videos, and elaborate set designs.

Lady Gaga sometimes expresses an idea to the Haus with collages made up of clippings from magazines and newspapers. She also uses word association and visual aids, such as landmarks, to get the scope of her ideas across. Members of the Haus then break into teams to invent and design until they capture Gaga's vision.

The Haus of Gaga helps Lady Gaga bring her vision for her fashion and performances such as this one to life.

A few of the Haus of Gaga's most famous inventions include the bubble dress she wore on the June 11, 2009, cover of *Rolling Stone* and iPod LCD glasses, which project images on little screens that are connected to an iPod. This invention was made famous in the video for "Poker Face." The Haus has also created light-up microphone gloves, hair-bow wigs, and the startlingly high heel-less hoof boots.

Throughout Lady Gaga's career, her style has changed, and the Haus of Gaga has adapted with the changes. This is because, as Haus makeup artist Sarah Tanno said, they are "always on the same wavelength ... our aesthetic of what we think is beautiful is very similar, which is why we work so well together."[19] Haus hair stylist Frederic Aspiras added, "We are like a family ... it is very sacred, and we are very protective of each other. But we're also pretty laid-back, and we're all so humble. In the tough times, we always have each other's shoulders to cry on. It's very special."[20]

The Haus on Tour

In addition to tech accessories and costume designs, the Haus also works tirelessly on complex set designs for Lady Gaga's live performances. Her elaborate sets for the Monster Ball tour were designed to give each audience the same experience, regardless of the size or location of the venue. When Lady Gaga described the stage design, she said, "Imagine you were to hollow out a TV and just break the fourth wall on a TV screen. It forces you to look at the center of the TV. It's my way of saying, 'My music is art.'"[21]

The Haus creates sets that offer layers of entertainment to give Lady Gaga's audience a complete performance art experience. They often project self-made short films onstage throughout Lady Gaga's shows and suit her in costumes that are part of the set. One such example is an enormous gyroscope called "the Orbit," in which Lady Gaga was surrounded by several moving rings.

Follow the Glitter Way

The elaborate Monster Ball tour was broken down into four acts, just like a play. It told a story, with each act delivering a component of the overall theme. Loosely based on *The Wizard of Oz*, the plot sent Lady Gaga and her dancer friends down Glitter Way to get to a party. Lady Gaga's entourage was moved along on their journey by her booming vocals and tightly choreographed dances. Each act had its own lavish set to conquer, but unlike Dorothy, who wants to get back home, Lady Gaga's goal is to arrive at the ultimate celebration—The Monster Ball. The New York City–themed acts, titled City, Subway, Forest, and Monster Ball, divided Lady Gaga's many hits among them.

The Haus of Gaga brought this elaborate storyline to life with jaw-dropping sets and high-tech gadgets and props. Each act of the show was separated by short films, written and directed by members of the Haus, that were projected on two giant video screens. The ambitious show included more than 15 costume changes for Lady Gaga and required around 24 semitrucks to haul all the equipment. Set design included the construction of a multilevel stage that was four times the size of the original stage Lady Gaga's team designed for the Fame Ball tour, a 40-foot (12 m) mechanical sea monster, a giant keyboard inside a hollowed-out car, and a tornado of fire above a piano.

The Monster Ball tour is a prime example of why Haus of Gaga–orchestrated concerts are often compared to a supercharged opera or musical theater. Music critics consistently validate that Lady Gaga is an entertainment visionary. As such, she is credited for having elevated concertgoers' expectations for live performances to an impossibly high level.

Advocate for LGBT+ People

Gaga mixes entertainment with politics, particularly issues of LGBT+ rights. She uses her star power to speak out against what she views as injustices toward the LGBT+ community. In turn, Lady Gaga's music, style, and outspoken dedication to LGBT+ rights have made her an icon for the current generation of LGBT+ people.

Gaga, who sometimes self-identifies as bisexual, has made it a priority to mainstream homosexuality. As she puts it, "I very much want to inject gay culture into the mainstream. It's not an

The Haus of Gaga helped bring Lady Gaga's massive Monster Ball tour to life. The elaborate tour involved four acts, each with its own theme.

underground tool for me. It's my whole life."[22] She invites Americans to reject social norms and let their true selves emerge—even if only at her concerts. She often announces at her shows that the "freaks" are outside the doors of the venue and that all of her Little Monsters are safe and loved and free to express themselves.

"Mother Monster," as Gaga is affectionately called by her fans, has a very public love affair with her LGBT+ fans. She repeatedly credits her LGBT+ fan base in interviews for her success. Before Gaga was selling out major concert venues, she played LGBT+ clubs in New York City. She reminds anyone with whom she partners that if they get onboard with Lady Gaga, they must be willing to get on board with LGBT+ culture. For example, when she and rapper Kanye West were considering touring together, she told him, "I'm gay. My music is gay. My show is gay. And I *love* that it's gay. And I love my gay fans and they're all going to be coming to our show. And it's going to *remain* gay."[23] Lady Gaga is a firm believer that LGBT+ people deserve the rights and privileges afforded to the heterosexual majority and should not be treated differently. Through her, they have a voice in mainstream culture, and she uses it to further two causes she feels passionately about: the right to marry and the right to serve openly in the military.

Same-Sex Marriage

Lady Gaga passionately believes same-sex couples should be afforded the right to marry, and she has used public appearances as opportunities to speak out in favor of same-sex marriage. In October 2009, Lady Gaga was invited to speak and perform at the Human Rights Campaign Dinner in Washington, D.C. President Barack Obama was also in attendance, and he opened his remarks by acknowledging Gaga's megastar status. "It is a privilege to be here tonight to open for Lady Gaga,"[24] he joked, and the crowd erupted in laughter. Before Lady Gaga launched into a performance of a revised version of John Lennon's "Imagine," she called on Obama to remember his campaign promises to the LGBT+ community. Lady Gaga and other supporters of same-sex marriage were disappointed when he did not immediately set out to work with Congress to repeal the Defense of Marriage Act (a law that defined marriage as a legal union between a man and a woman) as he promised when he ran for president in 2008.

Lady Gaga vocally supported same-sex marriage again at the National Equality March on Washington, D.C., also in October 2009. Before a crowd of tens of thousands of protestors, the LGBT+ rights activist shouted, "Obama we know you are listening. ARE YOU LISTENING? We will continue to push you and your administration to bring your words of promise to a reality. We need change now. We demand actions now."[25]

Lady Gaga and other supporters of same-sex marriage celebrated a serious victory when California's same-sex marriage ban, Proposition 8, was overturned on August 4, 2010. Lady Gaga was so overjoyed that she said she was immediately inspired to write a new song called "Future Love" about the struggle to achieve the right for same-sex couples to marry. On the day the ban was overturned, she tweeted, "At the moments notice of PROP 8 DEATH I instantly began to write music. BUBBLE DREAMS FOREVER! FULL EQUALITY! THIS IS JUST THE BEGININNG!"[26] She told Ryan Seacrest on his morning radio talk show that the decision felt like "a revolution,"[27] and that she had faith that same-sex marriage was a fight that could be won in all states. In June 2015, this fight was won when the U.S. Supreme Court made a landmark decision and ruled that same-sex couples could marry nationwide. Many people celebrated, including Lady Gaga. She posted on Twitter, "I can't stop crying. We did it kids."[28]

Repeal of Don't Ask, Don't Tell

In addition to same-sex marriage, Lady Gaga also threw her star power behind the movement to overturn the U.S. military's Don't Ask, Don't Tell (DADT) policy. The controversial legislation, introduced by President Bill Clinton in 1993, prohibited openly gay men and women from serving in the military. It also allowed investigations into service members' personal lives (to discover if they were gay or bisexual) in cases in which there was credible evidence of homosexuality.

Lady Gaga was outspoken about the need to repeal DADT. She showed her commitment to ending the ban on openly gay soldiers serving in the military when she brought four gay veterans as her dates to the 2010 MTV Video Music Awards. In a symbolic gesture, Gaga donned a dress and shoes made entirely of raw meat. She also carried a meat purse and wore a slab of meat on her head as a hat. She told Ellen DeGeneres in a September 13, 2010, interview that the dress symbolized oppression. She said to DeGeneres, "If we don't stand up for what we believe in and if we don't fight for our rights, pretty soon we're going to have as much rights as the meat on our own bones."[29]

Lady Gaga tweeted a message to ask Senate Majority Leader Harry Reid to call for a vote in the Senate to repeal DADT. She also posted a nearly eight-minute-long video on her website in which she called on members of the Senate to vote to debate a defense spending bill that included language that would overturn DADT. Lady Gaga also joined a rally in Portland, Maine, on September 20, 2010, where 2,000 protestors gathered to call on the state's two moderate Republican senators to vote to repeal DADT. In December 2010, the Don't Ask, Don't Tell Repeal Act of 2010 passed in both the House and Senate. The act was signed into law by President Obama on December 22, 2010, and took effect on September 20, 2011.

"Alejandro"

Other than showing her support for marginalized groups, another way that Lady Gaga uses her online presence is to generate great anticipation for her often controversial videos. She leaks information about the theme or content online but refuses to discuss details. Instead, she gives out bits of information to create a buzz of speculation. For example, the promotional buildup to the video for her hit song "Alejandro" went on for months. Lady Gaga and the Haus filmed previews and aired them on the internet as teasers. Long before the video was officially released, celebrity gossip columnists such as Perez Hilton heightened fans' anticipation with speculation about the video. They wondered what Lady Gaga would wear, who the director would be, and whether it would live up to Lady Gaga's earlier masterpieces.

Lady Gaga added to the "Alejandro" frenzy when she was interviewed for a live radio talk show in Australia. She steered the conversation toward her upcoming video and announced that they would soon begin filming. However, she refused to discuss any specifics. When she was asked about the content of the video, she exclaimed, "Are you absolutely mad? I would never, ever tell you! I would be more likely to lie through my teeth to you what the video's about so that you could all be surprised."[30] Of course, the hosts tried to pry the information out of her, but she changed the subject.

Her masterful media manipulation surrounding the "Alejandro" video release created a pop culture sensation when the music video finally aired on her website on June 8, 2010.

In 2010, Lady Gaga made waves by wearing a dress, shoes, and hat made entirely of raw beef. She wore the dress as a protest against the Don't Ask, Don't Tell policy.

Where Is the
Meat Dress Today?

After the 2010 MTV VMAs, the Rock and Roll Hall of Fame contacted Lady Gaga about what her plans for the meat dress were. Lady Gaga agreed to send it to the museum, but it was still raw meat, so they had to figure out how to preserve it. The museum landed on an idea that involved taxidermy and preserving it as though it was beef jerky. This is why the dress is not moldy, even years after the award show. According to Jun Francisco of the Rock and Roll Hall of Fame,

> *After the MTV event, the dress was taken to American Taxidermy in California and placed in a meat locker. It was then placed in a vat of chemicals and, while still pliable, was put on a body form and allowed to dry. This process actually took a while because the dress was made up of separate layers of Argentinian beef. After drying, the meat was painted to look fresh, rather than the dark, beef-jerky look it had taken when it began dehydrating.*[1]

The taxidermist sent the museum varieties of paint colors along with real pieces of meat to choose the appropriate paint color, and the museum chose the one that most matched the meat color from the night Lady Gaga wore it.

In 2015, the dress went on display at the museum in Cleveland, Ohio. However, before then, the dress was in a traveling Women Who Rock exhibit in connection with the museum. Francisco said they "transported it in a climate-controlled truck. It had its own crate that was made especially for it, and the case itself has its own temperature-controlled environment. Actually, it's not so much temperature as it is humidity. We have monitors inside that tells us the condition of the case and, yeah, the dress has held up pretty well."[2]

Francisco also covered another question: does the dress smell? Francisco stated the dress did not smell when they received it from the taxidermist and only smelled like the paint that was on it. Additionally, it is unsure how long the dress will last because nothing like this has been attempted before. In May 2019, the dress became part of a display at an exhibit called Haus of Gaga/Las Vegas in Las Vegas, Nevada.

1. Quoted in "Does Lady Gaga's Meat Dress Smell? (And Everything Else You Wanted to Know About the Dress!)," Rock and Roll Hall of Fame, September 11, 2015. www.rockhall.com/does-lady-gagas-meat-dress-smell-and-everything-else-you-wanted-know-about-dress.

2. Quoted in "Does Lady Gaga's Meat Dress Smell? (And Everything Else You Wanted to Know About the Dress!)," Rock and Roll Hall of Fame.

Lady Gaga's iconic meat dress was taxidermied for display at the Rock and Roll Hall of Fame in Cleveland, Ohio. The taxidermied dress and boots are shown here on display at a traveling exhibit.

Within the first few weeks of the video's release, it broke the record for the most-viewed video when it was watched more than 25 million times on YouTube.

Musical Collaborations

Another way Lady Gaga ensures a steady stream of publicity is through her collaborations with other artists, such as Beyoncé, RedOne, Akon, and Cyndi Lauper. She invests a lot of time and money in these collaborations and attributes her success, in part, to the relationships she has cultivated. Lady Gaga often collaborates with other artists and works closely with directors, dancers, and designers on the production of her videos. The release of each highly stylized concept video is controlled by her team and is meticulously promoted over time. The orchestration of such events requires Gaga to depend on a close network of trusted friends and colleagues. Together, they control how and when her videos are released, which means that she can count on a record-breaking number of viewers.

Lady Gaga has also struck up partnerships with companies such as Verizon, MAC Cosmetics, Polaroid, and Coca-Cola. Verizon and Coca-Cola products have appeared in her videos, Polaroid brought Lady Gaga on as its creative director, and MAC enlisted her as the face of a campaign. Around this time, several of her songs appeared in popular television shows, such as *Gossip Girl*, *The Hills*, and *Glee*. Lady Gaga also teamed up with the fragrance company Coty to develop her own line of perfumes. All of this cross-marketing benefits her record sales and also boosts the fame of those with whom she collaborates.

Her system of collaboration and cross-marketing worked well when she released the videos for "Poker Face," "Telephone," and "Bad Romance." Each video led to countless covers, parodies, and copycats. "Poker Face" was covered by artists such as Daughtry and Faith No More, and it was also spoofed by Eric Cartman on the animated series *South Park*. Soldiers in Afghanistan made a video tribute to "Telephone"

The "Gaga Episode"

"Bad Romance" spawned a number of tributes and parodies, but the biggest homage to the song occurred during a 2010 episode of the critically acclaimed television show *Glee*. Dubbed the "Gaga episode" by both the cast and fans, the cast performed a knockout rendition of "Bad Romance," which was hailed by critics as one of the show's greatest performances.

The characters dressed up in renditions of Gaga's most notorious costumes, including a bubble outfit and a dress made from Beanie Babies stuffed toys. The character Kurt wore a space-age silver dress, tights, and a version of the lobster-claw shoes that Gaga has worn. Other highlights of the episode included an acoustic version of "Poker Face" by the lead character Rachel and her mother. Gaga praised the episode on Twitter, saying, "GLEE WAS SO AMAZING! AH!!!!"[1] The cast of *Glee* was also pleased and cited "Bad Romance" and the Gaga episode in general when asked about their favorite moments from the show at Comic-Con International, also known as San Diego Comic-Con, in July 2010.

1. Lady Gaga, Twitter, May 26, 2010. twitter.com/ladygaga/status/14770658739.

in which they acted, lip-synched, danced, and dressed up in homemade Lady Gaga–esque costumes. The video was overwhelmingly popular and logged more than 5 million viewers on YouTube.

Lady Gaga's Charities

In addition to fighting for LGBT+ rights, Lady Gaga is also committed to several other causes and charities she cares deeply about. For example, Lady Gaga partnered with Virgin

Mobile, which was her tour sponsor, during the Monster Ball tour to help homeless youth. She pledged to match every dollar that was donated (up to $25,000) to Virgin Mobile's Re*Generation program.

Lady Gaga's Celebrity Fans

Lady Gaga's throng of fans, her Little Monsters, is a diverse bunch. She even counts many celebrities among some of her biggest fans. Jay-Z and Beyoncé Knowles are both admirers, to the point that Beyoncé collaborated with Lady Gaga on the single "Telephone." Elton John and Lady Gaga share a mutual admiration, and the two opened the 2010 Grammy Awards with a duet. Cyndi Lauper was an early and ardent Lady Gaga supporter, and the two do charity work together. Even Michael Jackson was rumored to be a Lady Gaga fan before his death in 2009. Lady Gaga revealed to Larry King that Jackson wanted her to open for him on his This Is It tour and even wanted to do duets onstage.

In addition, Lady Gaga and Virgin Mobile together offered VIP tickets to fans who volunteered with homeless youth organizations. The special ticket packages included a souvenir, special seating, and even the chance to meet Lady Gaga. The endeavor raised more than $80,000 and generated 30,000 hours of community service for hundreds of different homeless youth organizations across the country.

In January 2010, Lady Gaga took the opportunity to discuss another charitable venture during an interview with talk-show host Oprah Winfrey. Gaga begged viewers to help victims of the catastrophic 7.0 earthquake in Haiti that killed more than 230,000 people on January 12, 2010. The earthquake left more than 1 million people homeless and leveled more than a quarter of a million private homes and commercial buildings.

Lady Gaga announced on *The Oprah Winfrey Show*, Twitter, Facebook, and her website that 100 percent of the proceeds from ticket and merchandise sales from her January 24, 2010, concert at Radio City Music Hall would be donated to the earthquake relief fund. In addition, all the proceeds from merchandise sold on Lady Gaga's website on "Gaga for Haiti" day (January 24, 2010) was donated to earthquake victims. The effort raised more than $500,000 in one day.

MAC Cosmetics Campaign

In addition to her other charity work, Lady Gaga and pop star Cyndi Lauper were part of the Viva Glam campaign against AIDS and HIV. The campaign is a project of the MAC AIDS Fund; MAC is a high-end makeup company that sells Viva Glam lipstick and "lipglass." All proceeds from the Viva Glam lip line fund the MAC AIDS Fund. The fund provides money to help men, women, and children who have AIDS or who are HIV positive. The campaign raised more than $150 million.

Gaga, like her Viva Glam spokesperson predecessors, Boy George, RuPaul, and Lil' Kim, had her own colors in the Viva Glam lip line. She was featured in ads for the product and promoted the campaign in interviews and on her website. Money from the sale of the lipsticks provide education and services to people affected by HIV and AIDS. HIV is a disease that attacks the body's immune system and often advances to AIDS, which is deadly. Some of the services provided by the proceeds include counseling sessions for HIV-positive women, child care during doctor's appointments, boxes of nonperishable food, transportation for a month for women with HIV/AIDS to get to doctor's appointments, school supplies for kids orphaned by HIV/AIDS, and nutritional counseling for patients with HIV/AIDS.

Full Circle

In August 2010, Lady Gaga's career came full circle when she returned to Grant Park to perform at Lollapalooza. This time, however, she was a headliner. She brought her huge stage production with her. Perry Farrell, creator of the three-day festival that brought in about 90,000 people per day, said that Gaga's stage cost about $150,000 to build. He added that she was a natural

Lady Gaga is shown here performing at Lollapalooza in 2010. She was relatively unknown when she first performed at Lollapalooza in 2007, but when she returned the second time, her stage was massive and cost hundreds of thousands of dollars to build.

choice for the lineup: "I so appreciate someone who brings show. I mean, I'm building things just waiting for people like her. It's just natural. For Lollapalooza you've got the Chicago skyline and Lady Gaga. There it is."[31]

Just a few years into her career, there were many indications that Lady Gaga was in the music industry to stay. She had built a huge following made up of celebrities and average people alike and collaborated with major musicians such as Beyoncé on just her second album. Additionally, she was earning many award nominations and winning some of those awards, including Video of the Year for "Bad Romance." She had promised if she won that award that she would reveal the name of her next album, and she held up that promise. Thus, at the 2010 MTV VMAs, she revealed her next album was going to be called *Born This Way*, which was a phrase that meant a lot to many people, especially the LGBT+ community. The album also contained songs that held a lot of meaning. Around this time, Akon compared her to Michael Jackson, who was one of the most famous pop stars ever, and she was only three years into her career.

Chapter Four

Born Brave

When Lady Gaga announced her next album, *Born This Way*, at the 2010 VMAs, she gave away just a few details. She sang a bit of the chorus from the title song that was unreleased as of that time, and she said it was her greatest work to date. Lady Gaga said, "I'm so excited about it … the message, the melodies, the direction, the meaning, what it will mean to my fans and what it will mean to me in my own life—it's utter liberation. I'm on the quest to create the anthem for my generation for the next decade, so that's what I've done."[32] Lady Gaga had become an unstoppable, influential force in the music industry.

Born This Way

"It doesn't matter if you love him, or capital H-I-M / Just put your paws up 'cause you were born this way, baby."[33] The first single of Lady Gaga's *Born This Way* album starts out with these lyrics, and the song instantly became an anthem for so many. Lady Gaga had spent months teasing the album and song, and when it was finally released, the reception was mixed. Some felt overwhelmed with emotion and like they had a song that spoke to them. Others accused Lady Gaga of ripping off Madonna and criticized Lady Gaga's claims that she wrote the song in 10 minutes. Additionally,

Lady Gaga is shown here at a signing for her *Born This Way* album. Around this time, she also took her unique style a step further and debuted horned shoulder implants that were not real.

she received backlash from some members of the LGBT+ community, who stated that she was using them as a marketing tool.

However, the song meant a lot to many people, especially because Lady Gaga stated the song was an anthem for the LGBT+ community. Tim Cox, a fan of Lady Gaga's, said when he first heard the song live, he was overwhelmed and "broke down … I was hysterical with joy, with emotion—just completely lost

A Very Special Monster

Lady Gaga has a very special bond with all of her fans. However, there was one Little Monster who deeply affected her. In 2011, in Buffalo, New York, 14-year-old Jamey Rodemeyer died by suicide after extreme non-stop bullying from peers at his school. Jamey was a Lady Gaga fan, and he was gay. He regularly posted online about the endless bullying he was experiencing because of this and referenced Lady Gaga in many of his posts. However, the taunts from kids at school then moved online as well. Jamey posted "I always say how bullied I am, but no one listens. What do I have to do so people will listen to me?"[1] on September 9, 2011. On September 17, he quoted a lyric from Lady Gaga's song "The Queen" on his social media. On September 18, he posted a message to Lady Gaga on Twitter, telling her goodbye and thanking her. On that day, he died by suicide.

The news hit Lady Gaga, the LGBT+ community, and the Little Monsters hard. After learning of his death, Lady Gaga expressed her anger on Twitter and then did a tribute to Jamey at the iHeartRadio music festival. She had a video of Jamey on the screens behind her while she sang the song "Hair" from the *Born This Way* album. She said, "We lost a Little Monster this week … I wrote myself in the song."[34] Cox was frequently bullied in school and felt like something was wrong with him. He was also bullied for being gay. He is one of those fans who found a sense of community and belonging with other Lady Gaga fans. Therefore, when he heard "Born This Way" for the first time, it felt like a shield for him against the feelings he had of not being accepted. Cox said it was a shield "because you're not the one saying it anymore.

this record about how your identity is really all you've got when you're in school ... so tonight, Jamey, I know you're up there looking at us."[2]

Lady Gaga did not forget about this special Little Monster—she tweeted about him on the third anniversary of his death. Additionally, when she came to Buffalo on her artRAVE: The ARTPOP Ball tour in 2014, she brought his sister and her friend onstage while she sang "Born This Way" and put Jamey's name into her lyrics. Jamey's parents were also at the show, which she acknowledged during her set, and she expressed her love toward his family. Toward the end of the song, she asked the crowd to sing the next part loudly and put their hands up for Jamey because she was going to sing his favorite part of the album. She then sang the lyrics from "The Queen" that Jamey had posted before his death. Jamey's death brought national attention to bullying and suicide, and many people, including Lady Gaga, demanded that bullying be treated as a hate crime. Pop star Ricky Martin, who is also gay, voiced his outrage on Twitter and joined Lady Gaga in demanding an antibullying law be made in memory of Jamey.

1. Quoted in "Lady Gaga Sings Moving Tribute to Bullied Gay 14-Year-Old Who Committed Suicide as 500 Gather for Funeral," *Daily Mail*, September 26, 2011. www.dailymail.co.uk/news/article-2041622/Jamey-Rodemeyer-Lady-Gaga-sings-moving-tribute-gay-teen-committed-suicide.html.

2. Quoted in "Lady Gaga Sings Moving Tribute to Bullied Gay 14-Year-Old Who Committed Suicide as 500 Gather for Funeral."

Someone's defending you. And it's in a song that is playing on repeat on the radio, that everyone is talking about … All of a sudden, the idea that you were born this way and can't change who you are isn't just something that you feel: It's something the entire world is being forced to understand."[35]

In addition to the title track being an LGBT+ anthem, it also spoke to outsiders and anyone who felt like they did not fit in with the majority of society. The power of that song to speak to anyone who felt like an outsider is what gives it staying power. Additionally, what the song means to fans is why Lady Gaga does what she does—she is creating powerful, meaningful music that speaks to fans, not creating music for critics. This devotion to her fans is also evident in the tattoos she has dedicated to her Little Monsters.

Even though the title track and the album itself received criticism, the powerful pop throughout the whole album could not be ignored. The album spawned hits such as "The Edge of Glory," "Judas," "Marry the Night," and "Yoü and I," all of which showcased Lady Gaga's powerful voice.

Born This Way Foundation

The 2011 death of Lady Gaga fan Jamey Rodemeyer deeply affected the LGBT+ community and led to many demanding an antibullying law in his memory. In 2012, Lady Gaga and her mother created the Born This Way Foundation. The goal of the foundation is to create a kinder world through young people and provide them with resources and platforms to do that and make their voices heard. The foundation also implements evidence-based programming and works with young people to improve their communities and also improve mental health resources that are available to them. The foundation states on its website, "We launch programs tailored to and powered by young people, putting their ideas, voices, and needs first. We engage young people online and in their communities, working with a diverse group of partners to connect youth with the services they need to thrive and drive change."[36]

The Born This Way Foundation joined Lady Gaga on the Born This Way Ball throughout the tour. The foundation focuses on providing young people with the resources they need to help with mental health, bullying, and other issues.

The website for the Born This Way Foundation also includes resources for many issues young people may face, including body image issues, drug and alcohol abuse, bullying, depression, chronic pain, sexual abuse, and more. Lady Gaga experienced a lot of bullying when she was young. She was thrown in a trash can, called names, and deliberately excluded from things. In 2012, during the unveiling of the foundation at Harvard University, she did not want to talk as much about her own experiences with bullying because she did not want the foundation to only be about bullying. Lady Gaga's "aim is a far broader movement to change the culture and create a more supportive and tolerant environment."[37] She said, "The Born This Way Foundation is not restitution or revenge for my experiences ... I want to make that clear. This is: I am now a woman, I have a voice in the universe, and I want to do everything I can to become an expert in social justice and hope I can make a difference and mobilize young people to change the world."[38]

Born This Way Ball

In 2012, Lady Gaga set out to tour in support of the *Born This Way* album. Joining her on the tour was the Born Brave Bus. The bus was decorated by Little Monsters and offered professional private or group chats to talk about bullying, school, mental health, and more. The Born This Way Ball featured an elaborate stage that at that time was the largest scenic set that was ever built for touring. The set was designed by Lady Gaga and her creative team at the Haus of Gaga. Additionally, it took many months to build. The stage featured an enclosed area surrounded by a catwalk for lucky fans who had general admission tickets and arrived early. Additionally, the set featured a Gothic castle. The castle even had intricate carvings and other design work modeled after the medieval time period. Lady Gaga focuses on putting on an elaborate performance for her fans, and the Born This Way Ball was no exception. As this was the largest structure that was ever built for touring, her set required 15 different 53-foot (16 m) tractor trailers to transport the main stage as well as the castle.

In addition to an elaborate set, she also had elaborate costumes created by Armani, Versace, and Moschino. For each concert that she put on, there were an astounding 18 costume changes, which included a replica of the meat dress and an alien outfit. At one point in her set, she even became a human motorcycle.

Lady Gaga is known for giving a concert all of her energy. She puts on a stunning performance that leaves concertgoers

The Born Brave Bus could be seen on the Born This Way Ball tour. The bus was a place where fans could gather and have private or group chats with professionals about bullying and mental health, thus removing the stigma surrounding mental health.

astounded, and for many, it is the best show they have been to. This strenuous touring schedule and dance routine took its toll on Lady Gaga in February 2013, however. After postponing several tour dates because she was unable to walk, she had to cancel all the remaining concerts on the tour. After doctors performed tests to determine how severe the issue was, they discovered a labral tear of her right hip. It was determined she needed surgery and down time so that she could recover. While the cancellation of the tour was disappointing, fans did not have to wait long for Lady Gaga's next album.

Lady Gaga performed in a fake meat dress while on tour in 2012.

Backplane

In 2011, Backplane launched. This startup was Lady Gaga's revolutionary social network vision, and she dreamed of it as a place where online communities could be built. In particular, she viewed it as a place where Little Monsters could connect. The only community the network launched was the one for Little Monsters. It was a place for photo sharing and social media; however, the company never really took off, and it saw little success. Backplane started to crash, and in 2016, it went out of business.

ARTPOP

In November 2013, Lady Gaga's next album, *ARTPOP*, was released. The first single off the album, "Applause," featured a vibrant and catchy chorus. With what this song had to offer, fans and critics were wondering what the rest of the album would hold. However, the album flopped, and many viewed it as a disaster, or at least only half great. Many reviews pointed out that there were a few songs that were catchy, but the album overall missed the mark—or did it?

A 2016 revisiting of the album by *Billboard* magazine pointed out that it may have been perceived as a failure because of other albums surrounding *ARTPOP*'s release. That same fall, Beyoncé released a surprise album, and Miley Cyrus, Katy Perry, and Lorde released albums around that same time. That meant that "Applause" was often compared to Perry's "Roar" when it came to radio play, and it also had to go against powerful hits such as Cyrus's "Wrecking Ball" and Lorde's "Royals."

While *ARTPOP* has strong songs, such as "MANiCURE," critics pointed out that those songs were overshadowed by the poor decisions, public missteps, and poor marketing of the album. In the 2016 *Billboard* revisit of the album, Jason Lipshutz said,

> ARTPOP *does have obvious gems, but they were lost in the midst of a problematic rollout, right? The album era included an* ARTPOP *app that was confusing from the start, high-concept pairings with Jeff Koons and Marina Abramovic that didn't interest casual fans, performances at the VMAs that were more*

Lady Gaga is shown here at a 2014 tour performance for her *ARTPOP* album. Each concert featured many costume changes, and the first costume was this winged outfit.

kitschy than cool, and a disastrous "Do What U Want" video ...
that never saw the light of day ... even if you (like me) enjoyed
listen[ing] to "MANiCURE" and digging deep into the weirder
moments of the album, the public missteps were more glaring
than the underrated hooks.[39]

The second single on the album, "Do What U Want," featured R. Kelly and was well received. In fact, it was so well received that instead of "Venus" being the second single from the album, "Do What You Want" was put ahead of it because the song shot to number 1 on iTunes in 64 countries. In later years, Lady Gaga would acknowledge that she was not in a good place when she made the song and that she was trying to process the sexual abuse that she had experienced. In 2019, with R. Kelly facing a number of sexual misconduct charges, Lady Gaga apologized for this collaboration and pulled the song off all streaming services, stating that she would not work with him again.

Cheek to Cheek

In 2014, while touring on the artRAVE: The ARTPOP Ball tour, Lady Gaga released another album, this one an unexpected collaboration. The last few years were difficult for Lady Gaga, between canceling her tour, surgery, and the *ARTPOP* album not doing as well as her previous albums. In 2014, the classically trained singer toned down her image a bit and released an album with the iconic jazz and pop singer Tony Bennett, whom she met in 2011 for a collaboration on Bennett's *Duets II* record.

Cheek to Cheek features old jazz and pop standards such as the title track, "I Won't Dance," and "It Don't Mean a Thing (If It Ain't Got That Swing)." A review on the website Consequence of Sound stated, "Their voices complement each other and mesh together almost seamlessly."[40] Reviews also pointed out the power of Lady Gaga's voice and that it was easy to see how she sold out stadiums and inspired fans.

After a difficult few years and albums that did not live up to earlier works, many wondered where Lady Gaga would go in her

The artRAVE: The ARTPOP Ball had a massive stage design, much like Lady Gaga's previous tours. The stage was spread out among the floor area so that fans in areas farther from the stage were able to have a better view of Lady Gaga during portions of the concert.

career. Would she leave the industry? Would she bounce back better than ever? What she did end up doing astounded many; she not only released a new album, she also became a celebrated actress and Oscar winner.

Chapter **Five**

Actress, Singer, Icon

Lady Gaga had a rough few years, and in 2014, there was a lot of uncertainty surrounding her career. For the most part this uncertainty was from Lady Gaga herself. In 2014, she almost considered giving up pop music. At the end of that year, Lady Gaga's stylist asked her if she wanted to continue being a pop star. Lady Gaga told him, "You know, if I could just stop this train right now, today, I would. I just can't. [But] I need to get off now because I'm going to die." She added, "When you're going so fast you don't feel safe anymore, you feel like you're being slapped around and you can't think straight."[41] She cited the album with Tony Bennett as helping her to get through the tough time and reset her thinking. Additionally, she decided to only focus on projects that made her happy. This reset in her thinking resulted in a string of projects that led to her being an Oscar winner and having a series of concert shows, called a residency, in Las Vegas, Nevada.

American Horror Story

Lady Gaga's journey in focusing on projects that made her happy started with *American Horror Story*. The acclaimed TV show focuses on a new theme every season. The first season took place

In 2015, Lady Gaga became a much-loved cast member for two seasons of *American Horror Story*. She is shown here with the *Hotel* cast and crew.

in a haunted house, the second season was in an asylum, the third was about a witches' coven, the fourth was a carnival theme, and the fifth took place in a hotel. When it was announced that Lady Gaga would be taking on a starring role in *American Horror Story: Hotel*, many felt it was the perfect role for her. The show often pushes boundaries and does shocking things, and considering Lady Gaga's unique, eccentric performances, many thought she would fit right in.

In *American Horror Story: Hotel*, which aired in 2015, Lady Gaga played the Countess, who ran the hotel. The show received mixed reviews. Many praised Lady Gaga's performances, stating that the show did not feel like it was revolving around Lady Gaga as a person. A lot of the backlash against Lady Gaga was because she was not Jessica Lange, who had a starring role in the previous seasons but then left the show. Lange was a fan favorite, and it was hard for some fans to look beyond Lange and appreciate what Lady Gaga brought to the show. However, her hard work

Lady Gaga was determined to be a perfect fit for *American Horror Story*, and this was proven when she won a Golden Globe for her work on *American Horror Story: Hotel*.

was acknowledged when she won a Golden Globe for Best Actress in a Limited Series in 2016 for her work on *American Horror Story: Hotel*.

Show creator Ryan Murphy saw the potential Lady Gaga had and what she could bring to the show. Therefore, she ended up being a natural choice for a role in the 2016 season, *American Horror Story: Roanoke*. In this season, she played Scáthach, a witch who was the first Supreme, or head witch, of a coven. This would tie back around to the third season of the series, *Coven*.

"Til It Happens to You"

The Hunting Ground is a documentary about sexual assault on college campuses. It details the cover-ups of rape on college campuses as well as the toll it takes on the students and their families. Lady Gaga wrote a song for the film with Diane Warren, and it was a very personal one for both Warren and Lady Gaga as they are both survivors of sexual assault. At 19 years old, Lady Gaga was sexually assaulted by a record producer. She put a lot of her personal experiences into the song, and she credits Warren with helping her. Lady Gaga said, "Diane had to convince me that it was okay to sing about this and reveal this thing about myself."[1] Lady Gaga performed the song at the 2016 Oscars, and "the performance climactically ended with a group of sexual assault survivors surrounding Gaga at the piano with the words 'Not Your Fault' written on their arms."[2]

1. Quoted in Mia Galuppo, "Lady Gaga on Her Song 'Til It Happens to You': 'I Wanted It to Be Empowering,'" *Billboard*, January 6, 2016. www.billboard.com/articles/columns/pop/6835256/lady-gaga-til-it-happens-to-you-empowering.

2. Brittany Spanos, "Lady Gaga Delivers Powerful 'Til It Happens to You' at Oscars 2016," *Rolling Stone*, February 29, 2016. www.rollingstone.com/tv/tv-news/lady-gaga-delivers-powerful-til-it-happens-to-you-at-oscars-2016-111784/.

Lady Gaga received such praise for her work in the show that fans were wondering if she would be returning for a third season. As of summer 2019, there were no plans for her to return to the show.

Joanne

The year 2016 was a busy one for Lady Gaga. In addition to another starring role in *American Horror Story*, she released an album, prepared for her Super Bowl halftime show, supported Hillary Clinton's run for president, and filmed a documentary.

Lady Gaga's album *Joanne*, released in October 2016, took

Lady Gaga's style changed drastically with the *Joanne* album. She was often seen wearing a pink hat, and the cover of the album also depicts her wearing the pink hat.

on a much more personal tone for her, and it also took on a new sound. This album was more stripped down and restrained than previous albums, which was particularly evident in the title track. The album is named after Lady Gaga's aunt, Joanne Germanotta, who was her father's sister. Joanne died from complications from the autoimmune disease lupus before Lady Gaga was even born. Joanne was only 19. Lady Gaga said, "*Joanne* is about living every day as if it's my last … My father's sister died when she was 19—that was Joanne, my aunt. This was the center of the pain in my family. Growing up, I never understood what the tears of my family were about."[42] Lady Gaga said when she first played the song for her father, it brought tears to his eyes.

In addition to this deeply personal song, the album includes a duet called "Hey Girl" with Florence Welch of the band Florence and the Machine, as well as a song called "Perfect Illusion." "Perfect Illusion" was the first single from the album, and it displays Lady Gaga's powerful vocals as she belts out the chorus. The release of the song also had fans questioning if it was more personal than she was admitting—two months prior to the release of the album, Lady Gaga had ended her engagement to actor Taylor Kinney. The couple had been together for five years, since 2011, when they met on the set of the "Yoü and I" music video. Lady Gaga said that "Perfect Illusion" was about dating in the digital age and how people portray themselves on the internet—nobody knows what to believe about the other person because it could be a lie. The music video for the song was not choreographed or rehearsed at all—Lady Gaga simply did what she felt in the moment.

Five Foot Two

Shortly after the release of *Joanne*, Lady Gaga had an important and massive performance in February 2017: she performed during the halftime show at the Super Bowl. Lady Gaga's set has been listed as one of the top halftime shows by CBS Sports and *Sports Illustrated*, and rightfully so—she made a grand entrance by jumping off the roof down to the stage,

Lady Gaga put on a thrilling Super Bowl halftime show performance, which started off with her jumping off the roof onto the stage.

making one of the most memorable entrances in Super Bowl halftime show history to date. She did aerial acrobatics over the stage, which was massive—as her stages often are. Lady Gaga started out the set singing patriotic songs and then went into hits such as "Poker Face," "Born This Way," "Telephone," "Bad Romance," and "Million Reasons." Even though the set was short, Lady Gaga still put on the show as though it was a full concert on her tour. Her show included plenty of dancers, fire, and lighting effects. Her talent and skills were on display for millions, and she put on an entertaining show that set a standard for halftime shows.

The making of the *Joanne* album and the Super Bowl halftime show were also detailed in the Netflix documentary *Gaga: Five Foot Two*. The documentary follows Lady Gaga throughout deeply personal events beyond her career. It also detailed how her career affected her personal life. One emotional moment in the documentary shows Lady Gaga crying because of problems she was having with her fiancé at the time and how her career tends to end her relationships. In addition to seeing this side of Lady Gaga, her struggles with chronic pain are a major theme throughout the film. Lady Gaga has fibromyalgia, which causes people to feel pain in their tendons and muscles, and they often also have sleep problems or headaches. Many people believe fibromyalgia is not a real disorder, and Lady Gaga is trying to remove the stigma surrounding this disorder as well as around mental health problems. She said,

> I get so irritated with people who don't believe fibromyalgia is real…for me, and I think for many others, it's really a cyclone of anxiety, depression, PTSD, trauma, and panic disorder, all of which sends the nervous system into overdrive, and then you have nerve pain as a result…People need to be more compassionate. Chronic pain is no joke. And it's every day waking up not knowing how you're going to feel.[43]

Some people with chronic pain applauded Lady Gaga coming out about her struggles in such a visible way because of the power of her celebrity status. When celebrities speak out in support of or against something, people listen. Lady Gaga speaking out about a disorder that many people believe is not real is an important step in removing stigma surrounding invisible illnesses.

Jackson and Ally

A documentary is not the only film Lady Gaga has under her belt. In 2018, the critically acclaimed movie *A Star Is Born* was released, starring her and Bradley Cooper in the lead roles of Ally and Jackson Maine. Cooper first spent time with Lady Gaga in 2016 after a benefit where she sang "La Vie en Rose." After hearing her sing, he knew he wanted that song in the version of *A Star Is Born* that he was directing. (Lady Gaga and Cooper's version of the movie is the fourth time it has been made.) He wanted to meet her and immediately got in contact with her agent. He met her right away at her home, she made him pasta, and they immediately had a connection. He knew that there was no one else he wanted in the lead role of Ally, but it took a lot to convince Warner Bros., the company financing the film, of what Cooper already knew. Several screen tests had to be done, one of which involved Cooper wiping off all of Lady Gaga's makeup because he wanted her to have a natural look in the film. He wanted Stefani Germanotta, not the pop star Lady Gaga. He stood by her, believing 100 percent in casting her and eventually, he got his wish. Lady Gaga said, "There could be 100 people in the room and 99 don't believe in you. You just need one—and it was him."[44] Cooper has also said, "I can't imagine having the courage to do it without her…No actress can do musically what I needed Stefani to do in 42 days of shooting: I needed plutonium. And the plutonium in *A Star Is Born* is Stefani's voice."[45]

Cooper's instinct to cast Lady Gaga was correct, and the positive reviews pouring in after the movie's debut proved that. *Rolling Stone* gave the movie 4.5 out of 5 stars, crediting the raw, lived-in feeling of the movie instead of it feeling like a glamorous, polished story. Fans and critics responded well

Bradley Cooper fully believed in and supported Lady Gaga's casting in the lead role of Ally in *A Star Is Born*. He fought to have her cast in the movie, even when the production company doubted him. The casting was spot on, and the movie was widely acclaimed. The pair are seen here promoting the movie at a film festival.

"I'll Never Love Again"

"I'll Never Love Again" is a very emotional part of the movie *A Star Is Born*. Lady Gaga's performance of the song earned rave reviews because of how emotionally raw it was, and it was a difficult scene for her to film. That is because the emotion behind it was completely real for her. Right before Lady Gaga had to film that scene, she got a call that her best friend, Sonja Durham, who had stage IV cancer, was about to pass away. Lady Gaga immediately got into her car to see her, but Sonja passed away 10 minutes before she arrived. She stayed with her friend's family for a while, not knowing what to do. Sonja's husband told her Sonja would want her to go back to work and sing, and within that hour, she went back to the set and filmed the final song of *A Star Is Born*.

to the central love story of the movie. This was especially evident in Cooper and Lady Gaga's duet "Shallow." The song won a Golden Globe and a Grammy in 2019. It also won an Oscar, adding this prestigious award to Lady Gaga's collection. Additionally, the soundtrack, which features songs by Lady Gaga and Cooper, surpassed more than 1 million copies sold in the United States in March 2019. New fans and Little Monsters responded well to many songs on the album, such as Cooper's "Maybe It's Time"; "Music to My Eyes," which is a duet between Cooper and Lady Gaga; and "Always Remember Us This Way" and "I'll Never Love Again," both of which were sung by Lady Gaga.

The connection and chemistry between Cooper and Lady Gaga caught the attention of fans, journalists, and critics around the world. The two credit their trust and close

Lady Gaga arrived at the 2019 Met Gala in a large pink cloak, shown here. Underneath the cloak, she had on three additional outfits and made a performance out of revealing them.

friendship with the intimacy of their performances on screen. Fans became especially enamored with their relationship after the two performed "Shallow" at the 2019 Oscars. Many people believed that moment was the highlight of the telecast because of how well it showed off both their voices and their chemistry.

Enigma

In 2018, Lady Gaga started her concert residency in Las Vegas, Nevada. This means she performs all of her concerts from this specific venue. Additionally, as it is a two-year residency, which means many fans will have the opportunity to see her, whereas a tour may last only a few months. There are two different versions of the show. One, called Enigma, features Lady Gaga's hits in a new concert experience. The second version is Lady Gaga Jazz and Piano, which features stripped-down versions of her songs and classic jazz and swing songs. Lady Gaga said of the show, "We're creating a show unlike anything I've done before. It will be a celebration of all that is unique and different within us. The challenges of bravery can be overcome with creativity and courage that is grown out of adversity, love and music."[46]

Lady Gaga worked incredibly hard to get to where she is today. From studying performing arts in school to making the decision to leave college and pursue a music career full-time to working her way up in the music industry to get her first album out there, she is a symbol of perseverance and hard work. She made a name for herself in the music industry, showing that she had incredible talent to take her far and succeed beyond her first album—in 2019, she was teasing a sixth one on Twitter. In the more than 10 years of her career to date, she has released an astounding variety of music with each song sounding different from anything else she has done. She puts on entertaining shows, whether it is a nearly 15-minute set at the Super Bowl or a 2-hour concert. She is a Grammy, Golden Globe, and Oscar winner. She is an acclaimed actress whom Bradley Cooper believed in and the only one he wanted in the lead role in his first movie as a director. Lady Gaga is an inspiration to many, a celebrity voice giving representation to marginalized groups and removing stigma from mental illness. On top of all of this, she is still the Mother Monster to her fans.

Notes

Introduction: Mother Monster

1. Bradley Cooper, dir. *A Star Is Born*. Burbank, CA: Warner Bros. Pictures, 2018.

2. Quoted in Kate Beaudoin, "The Story of How Lady Gaga Became Famous Will Make You Like Her Even More," Mic, March 10, 2015. mic.com/articles/112334/the-story-of-how-lady-gaga-became-famous-will-make-you-like-her-even-more#.ybPD2QUG2.

Chapter One: The Star Is Born

3. Quoted in Jonathan Borge, "Lady Gaga's Mom on Her Daughter's Mental Health Struggles," *InStyle*, May 7, 2018. www.instyle.com/news/lady-gaga-mom-cynthia-germanotta-motherhood-interview.

4. Quoted in Borge, "Lady Gaga's Mom on Her Daughter's Mental Health Struggles."

5. Quoted in Vanessa Grigoriadis, "Growing Up Gaga," *New York*, March 28, 2010. nymag.com/arts/popmusic/features/65127.

6. Quoted in Grigoriadis, "Growing Up Gaga."

7. Quoted in Nicholas Kristof, "Born to Not Get Bullied," *New York Times*, February 29, 2012. www.nytimes.com/2012/03/01/opinion/kristof-born-to-not-get-bullied.html.

8. Quoted in Lucille Barilla, "Lady Gaga Talks About Her 9/11 Experience," SheKnows, September 11, 2011. www.sheknows.com/entertainment/articles/841021/lady-gaga-talks-her-9-11-experience/.

9. Quoted in Neil McCormack, "Lady Gaga: 'I've Always Been Famous and You Just Didn't Know It,'" *Telegraph*, February 16, 2010. www.telegraph.co.uk/culture/music/rockandpopfeatures/7221051/Lady-Gaga-Ive-always-been-famous-you-just-didnt-know-it.html.

10. Quoted in John Seabrook, "Transformer," *New Yorker*, February 1, 2010. www.newyorker.com/talk/2010/02/01/100201ta_talk_seabrook.

Chapter Two: *The Fame Monster*

11. Quoted in Craig Marks, "Producer Rob Fusari Dishes on Lady Gaga, Beyoncé," *Billboard*, February 24, 2010. www.billboard.com/features/producer-rob-fusari-dishes-on-lady-gaga1004070301.story#/features/producer-rob-fusari-dishes-on-lady-gaga-1004070301.story?page=1.

12. Quoted in Cortney Harding, "Lady Gaga: The Billboard Cover Story," *Billboard*, August 7, 2009. www.billboard.com/features/lady-gaga-the-billboard-cover-story-1004001347.story?page=2#/features/lady-gaga-the-billboard-cover-story-1004001347.story?page=3.

13. Quoted in Ryan Pearson, "Akon: Lady Gaga Made Me Rich," *Huffington Post*, February 17, 2010. www.huffingtonpost.com/2010/02/17/akon-lady-gaga-made-me-ri_n_465641.html.

14. Quoted in Harding, "Lady Gaga."

15. Jill Menze, "Lady Gaga/May 2, 2009/New York/(Terminal 5)," *Billboard*, May 4, 2009. www.billboard.com/bbcom/reviews-live/lady-gaga-may-2-2009-new-york-terminal-5-1003969033.story#/bbcom/reviews-live/lady-gaga-may-2-2009-new-york-terminal-5-1003969033.story.

16. David Drake, "Top 100 Tracks of 2009," Pitchfork, December 14, 2009. pitchfork.com/features/staff-lists/7742-the-top-100-tracks-of-2009/7.

17. Lady Gaga, Twitter, February 2, 2010. twitter.com/ladygaga/status/8561296471.

Chapter Three: A Charitable and Fashionable Star

18. Quoted in Rachel Dodes, "Lady Gaga Was Alexander McQueen's 'Unofficial Muse,'" *Wall Street Journal*, February 11, 2010. blogs.wsj.com/runway/2010/02/11/lady-gaga-was-mcqueens-unofficial-muse.

19. Quoted in Sharon Kanter, "Inside Lady Gaga's Glam Style Squad, the Haus of Gaga: 'We Are Like a Family,'" *People*, February 13, 2019. people.com/style/lady-gaga-haus-of-gaga-details/.

20. Quoted in Kanter, "Inside Lady Gaga's Glam Style Squad, the Haus of Gaga: 'We Are Like a Family.'"

21. Quoted in Jocelyn Vena and Sway Calloway, "Lady Gaga Plans to Battle Her 'Monsters' During Monster Ball Tour," MTV News, November 6, 2009. www.mtv.com/news/articles/1625651/20091105/lady_gaga.jhtml.

22. Quoted in Joshua David Stein and Noah Michelson, "The Lady Is a Vamp," *Out*, September 2009. www.out.com/exclusives.asp?id=25701.

23. Quoted in Stein and Michelson, "The Lady Is a Vamp."

24. Barack Obama, "Remarks by the President at Human Rights Campaign Dinner," White House, October 11, 2009. obamawhitehouse.archives.gov/realitycheck/the-press-office/remarks-president-human-rights-campaign-dinner.

25. Quoted in Michael Solis, "Lady Gaga and Obama for Gay America," *Huffington Post*, August 22, 2010. www.huffingtonpost.com/michael-solis/lady-gaga-and-obama-for-g_b_318088.html.

26. Lady Gaga, Twitter, August 4, 2010. twitter.com/ladygaga/status/20350379949.

27. Quoted in Ryan Seacrest, "Lady Gaga Explains Going Crowd Surfing at Lollapalooza," RyanSeacrest.com, August 11, 2010. www.ryanseacrest.com/blog/whats-happening/lady-gaga-explains-going-crowd-surfing-at-lollapalooza-audio.

28. Quoted in "Celebrities React to Supreme Court Gay Marriage Ruling," *Chicago Tribune*, June 26, 2015. www.chicagotribune.com/entertainment/ct-gay-marriage-ruling-celeb-reaction-20150626-htmlstory.html.

29. Quoted in "Lady Gaga Is Victorious at the VMAs!," *The Ellen DeGeneres Show*, September 13, 2010. ellen.warnerbros.com/2010/09/lady_gaga_is_victorious_at_the_vmas_vod_0913.php.

30. Quoted in Ryan, Monty, and Wippa, "Lady Gaga Chats to Her 'Little Monsters,'" Nova 96.9 FM, March 23, 2010. www.novafm.com.au/Audio.aspx?id=96892&site=Nova969&s=78.

31. Quoted in Angela Watercutter, "Perry Farrell: Lady Gaga Was My Lollapalooza Marble," *Wired*, June 8, 2010. www.wired.com/underwire/2010/06/perry-farrell-lollapalooza.

Chapter Four: Born Brave

32. Quoted in Kara Warner, "Lady Gaga Announces *Born This Way* Album at VMAs," MTV, September 13, 2010. www.mtv.com/news/1647696/lady-gaga-announces-born-this-way-album-at-vmas/.

33. Lady Gaga, "Born This Way," *Born This Way,* Interscope, 2011.

34. Quoted in Lynn Neary, "How 'Born This Way' Was Born: An LGBT Anthem's Pedigree," NPR, January 30, 2019. www.npr.org/2019/01/30/687683804/lady-gaga-born-this-way-lgbt-american-anthem.

35. Quoted in Neary, "How 'Born This Way' Was Born: An LGBT Anthem's Pedigree."

36. "About the Foundation," Born This Way Foundation. bornthisway.foundation/about-the-foundation/.

37. Kristof, "Born to Not Get Bullied."

38. Quoted in Kristof, "Born to Not Get Bullied."

39. Joe Lynch and Jason Lipshutz, "'ARTPOP' Revisited: Arguing the Pros & Cons of Lady Gaga's Challenging Third Album," *Billboard*, October 25, 2016. www.billboard.com/articles/columns/pop/7556753/lady-gaga-artpop-revisited-merits.

40. Katherine Flynn, "Lady Gaga and Tony Bennett—Cheek to Cheek," Consequence of Sound, September 26, 2014. consequenceofsound.net/2014/09/album-review-lady-gaga-and-tony-bennett-cheek-to-cheek/.

Chapter Five: Actress, Singer, Icon

41. Quoted in Lynsey Eidell, "Lady Gaga Reveals the Surprising Reason She Almost Quit Pop Music," *Glamour*, December 4, 2015. www.glamour.com/story/lady-gaga-almost-quit-pop-music.

42. Ashley Iasimone, "Lady Gaga Opens Up About Her Aunt Joanne's Lupus Battle in V Magazine," *Billboard*, August 28, 2017. www.billboard.com/articles/columns/pop/7942384/lady-gaga-v-magazine-cover-aunt-joanne-lupus-album.

43. Quoted in Laura Hensley, "Lady Gaga on Her Fight with Fibromyalgia: 'Chronic Pain Is No Joke,'" Global News, September 22, 2018. globalnews.ca/news/4438236/what-is-fibromyalgia-lady-gaga/.

44. Quoted in Amy Mackelden, "Everything You Need to Know About Lady Gaga & Bradley Cooper's Working Relationship," *Harper's Bazaar*, February 28, 2019. www.harpersbazaar.com/celebrity/latest/a26142499/lady-gaga-bradley-cooper-relationship-timeline/.

45. Quoted in Mackelden, "Everything You Need to Know About Lady Gaga & Bradley Cooper's Working Relationship."

46. Quoted in Melinda Newman, "The Forever Enigmatic Lady Gaga," MGM Resorts. www2.mgmresorts.com/ladygaga/.

Lady Gaga Year by Year

1986

Stefani Joanne Angelina Germanotta is born on March 28 to Joseph and Cynthia Germanotta.

1990

Stefani learns to play the piano by ear when she is just four years old.

1992

Stefani plays her first piano recital at the exclusive Convent of the Sacred Heart Academy in Manhattan.

1999

Stefani writes her first piano ballad, "To Love Again."

2001

The September 11, 2001, attacks on New York and Washington, D.C., leave a lasting impression on the 15-year-old.

2002

Stefani records her first demo.

2003

Stefani is one of only twenty students admitted for early acceptance that year to the prestigious Tisch School of the Arts at New York University.

2005

Stefani drops out of Tisch to begin pursuing a music career full-time and begins performing with the SGBand (Stefani Germanotta Band).

2006

Singer and talent scout Wendy Starland sees the SGBand perform and introduces Germanotta to producer Rob Fusari. The two begin working on songs together, and Stefani changes her stage name to Lady Gaga. She is briefly signed to Def Jam Recordings but is quickly dropped and gets a contract shortly thereafter with Interscope Records. Lady Gaga meets Lady Starlight in March and signs a music publishing deal with Sony/ATV Music Publishing. She will eventually write songs for Britney Spears, New Kids on the Block, and more.

2007

Lady Gaga and Lady Starlight begin performing as Lady Gaga and the Starlight Revue. Their performances gain them some notoriety, and they play Chicago's Lollapalooza music festival in August. Lady Gaga's performance receives mostly positive reviews. She eventually sings a guide vocal for producer/performer Akon, and he recognizes her potential. Akon obtains permission from Interscope to sign Lady Gaga to his label, Kon Live Distribution.

2008

Lady Gaga records *The Fame* early in the year. The first single, "Just Dance," is released on April 8 and becomes an instant dance club anthem. The full album is released on August 19. Lady Gaga also performs as the opening act for label mates New Kids on the Block during their 2008 tour.

2009

Lady Gaga kicks off her first solo world tour, the Fame Ball, at the House of Blues in San Diego on March 12. *The Fame Monster*, an eight-track EP of entirely new Lady Gaga material, is released on November 18. Lady Gaga announces the Monster Ball tour in October 2009 to replace the canceled Fame Kills tour she was to coheadline with Kanye West. The Monster Ball tour begins on November 27 in Montreal, Canada. Lady Gaga gives a memorable performance of "Paparazzi" at the 2009 MTV Video Music Awards and wins an award for Best New Artist. "Paparazzi" wins awards for Best Art Direction and Best Special Effects.

2010

The video for "Alejandro" is released on June 8. In August, Lady Gaga is nominated for a record 13 MTV Video Music Awards for the "Bad Romance" and "Telephone" videos; she returns to Lollapalooza, this time as a headliner. In September, she wins eight MTV Video Music Awards, including Video of the Year for "Bad Romance." Lady Gaga also is the keynote speaker at a rally to repeal the Don't Ask, Don't Tell policy in Portland, Maine.

2011

Born This Way is released and spawns singles including the title track, "Judas," "Edge of Glory," "Marry the Night," and more; she starts dating Taylor Kinney. The death of Lady Gaga fan Jamey Rodemeyer sparks outrage among Lady Gaga, Little Monsters, and the LGBT+ community. Lady Gaga starts demanding an antibullying law in memory of Jamey.

2012

Lady Gaga embarks on the Born This Way Ball tour.

2013

Lady Gaga sustains a hip injury from strenuous touring and dance routines and has to get surgery to repair the damage. She cancels the remaining dates of the Born This Way Ball tour in order to receive the surgery and recover and then releases the *ARTPOP* album.

2014

Lady Gaga tours in support of the *ARTPOP* album and releases an album of jazz and pop songs called *Cheek to Cheek* with Tony Bennett.

2015

Lady Gaga stars as the Countess in *American Horror Story: Hotel*.

2016

Lady Gaga stars as Scáthach in *American Horror Story: Roanoke*; she releases *Joanne*; and she breaks up with Taylor Kinney.

2017

Lady Gaga plays the Super Bowl halftime show, and she releases the documentary Gaga: *Five Foot Two*.

2018

Lady Gaga stars in *A Star Is Born* with Bradley Cooper and starts her Las Vegas, Nevada, residency tour Enigma.

2019

Lady Gaga wins a Golden Globe, Oscar, and Grammy for "Shallow" from *A Star Is Born*; breaks up with fiancé Christian Carino; and teases sixth album.

For More Information

Books

Fielder, Hugh. *Lady Gaga: A Monster Romance*. London, UK: Flame Tree Publishing, 2012.
Fielder's book features a biography on Lady Gaga along with photos and quotes from the pop star.

Goodman, Elizabeth. *Lady Gaga: Critical Mass Fashion*. New York, NY: St. Martin's Griffin, 2010.
This book catalogs Lady Gaga's outrageous fashions, showcasing the creations of the Haus of Gaga as well as the designs of Alexander McQueen and other fashion masters.

Herbert, Emily. *Lady Gaga: Behind the Fame*. New York, NY: Overlook, 2010.
This book presents an overview of Lady Gaga's life from her childhood up to the release of *The Fame Monster*.

Lady Gaga and Terry Richardson. *Gaga*. New York, NY: Grand Central Publishing, 2011.
This collaboration between Lady Gaga and Richardson features full-color photographs of the singer.

Morgan, Johnny. *Gaga*. New York, NY: Sterling, 2010.
This book features full-color photographs of Lady Gaga along with a biography of the star.

Websites

Born This Way Foundation
(bornthisway.foundation)
Started by Lady Gaga and her mother, the foundation helps young
  adults and provides information on mental health resources,
  bullying, gender, self-care, and more.

Lady Gaga: Official Website
(www.ladygaga.com)
This is the official place on the web for all things Lady Gaga.

Lady Gaga on Facebook
(www.facebook.com/ladygaga/)
The official Facebook page of Lady Gaga allows fans to stay
  updated on her upcoming tours, albums, and movies.

Lady Gaga on Instagram
(www.instagram.com/ladygaga)
Lady Gaga's Instagram page allows fans to keep up with her
  daring style, tours, and more.

Lady Gaga on Twitter
(twitter.com/ladygaga)
Lady Gaga's official Twitter page is regularly updated with
  information on albums, tours, and more.

Index

Picture Credits

Cover Andrea Raffin/Shutterstock.com; p. 7 Dominick Reuter/ AFP/Getty Images; pp. 9, 43 s_bukley/Shutterstock.com; p. 10 Valerie Macon/AFP/Getty Images; p. 14 Kevin Mazur/Getty Images; pp. 17, 25 Theo Wargo/WireImage/Getty Images; p. 18 Christopher Polk/Getty Images for Children's Mending Hearts; p. 20 (left) Samuel Kubani/AFP/Getty Images; p. 20 (right) Oli Scarff/Getty Images; p. 23 Monica Schipper/Getty Images; p. 27 Daniel Boczarski/Redferns/Getty Images; p. 31 John Medina/ WireImage/Getty Images; pp. 33 Jason Merritt/Getty Images; p. 35 Christopher Polk/Getty Images; p. 37 Lester Cohen/WireImage/ Getty Images; p. 39 (main) JStone/Shutterstock.com; pp. 39 (inset), 76 Kathy Hutchins/Shutterstock.com; p. 44 Tinseltown/ Shutterstock.com; p. 46 Tim Mosenfelder/Getty Images; p. 49 Barry King/WireImage/Getty Images; pp. 53, 77 Featureflash Photo Agency/Shutterstock.com; p. 55 Jewel Samad/AFP/Getty Images; pp. 60, 63, 72 Kevin Mazur/WireImage/Getty Images; p. 67 Gilbert Carrasquillo/Getty Images; p. 69 David Livingston/ Getty Images; p. 70 VCG/VCG via Getty Images; p. 74 Paul Kane/WireImage/Getty Images; p. 79 Behrouz Mehri/AFP/ Getty Images; p. 81 Timothy A. Clary/AFP/Getty Images; p. 84 Denis Makarenko/Shutterstock.com; p. 86 Neilson Barnard/ Getty Images.

About the Author

Nicole Horning has been a fan of Lady Gaga's since "Just Dance" was released and has wanted to write a book on Lady Gaga for years. Nicole holds a bachelor's degree in English and a master's degree in education from D'Youville College in Buffalo, New York. She lives in Western New York with her cats, Khaleesi and Evie, and writes and reads in her free time.